Organizational
Synergy

A Practical Guide

Recalibrate Interactions To Achieve Peak
Engagement, Productivity & Profit

by
Dr. Rami Ben-Yshai

This book is dedicated with love to my daughters Nufar and Carmel, the most wonderfully synergistic creation in my life. Thank you for all you taught me, for your love, and for being with me, no matter what narratives life spun for us.

"*This book methodically and clearly describes all forms of interaction* which may exist in any company. Special emphasis is placed on synergy: when it can develop, and how it can be achieved from any of these interactive relationships. After I read the book, **the term "synergy" changed from being an abstract vision to a viable objective.** I was able to define goals and create the processes for achieving it in our company."
Ayala Garon, Quality Processes Manager, DSIT – producers of sonar and security systems.

*

"*This book presents fascinating questions to consultants: what is organizational synergy, is it always correct to aim for it, what costs might it entail, and is cooperation and containment necessary in order to assimilate it. However,* **the book's greatest contribution is in offering the 7 Forms of Interaction Model.** *On the very day I read the book , the model helped me establish concrete order in a consultancy situation. I warmly recommend that everyone studies this wonderful tool available to us.*"
Dr. Ora Setter, Senior Organizational Consultant & Training Manager, Israel Organizational Development Association.

*

"*Dr. Rami Ben-Yshai provides a clear presentation of the tools and process for creating effective synergy among your organization's departments, and between organizations wishing to cooperate for improved outcomes. I greatly appreciated his approach, which emphasizes growth derived from interpersonal differences,* **foregoing the negative elements of ego, and integrating forces on the way to business success.**"
Gil Peretz, author of "WOW" and international lecturer on leadership, influence and peak performance.

*

"*Implementing the synergy principles taught by Rami saved me precious management time, pushed the company forward, and promoted the personal and professional development of my team. Dr. Rami ben-Yshai is not only a fascinating speaker and senior organizational consultant but uses his rich experience to convey content in clear, practical terms. I warmly recommend the book.*"
Dr. Yaniv Zeid, Attorney

"**Rami forged team spirit in a unique fashion.** We learned to give space to diversity, which actually encourages linking between managers. Rami assisted us greatly: this is the first time I felt comfortable about being away on a business trip abroad, knowing that things would be working okay even when I was physically absent."
Doron Bakchy, CEO, Bringoz

*

"Rami was with us every step of the way, advising throughout the merger which eventuated in the "Ziv, Shifer & Co." accountancy firm. **The cooperation Rami made possible between the two offices improved organizational culture and profits.** The synergy Rami created produced what synergy should: the whole was greater than the parts. This book, which was still in production at the time, tangibly presents the perception, tools and working processes needed for a successful merger.
Reading this book several years after the merger's completion let me evaluate our achievements since then and recalibrate to the current reality. The book can greatly assist anyone considering the merger process."
Yoram Shiffer, CPA, managing partner in Ziv, Shifer & Co. Accountancy

*

"In urban planning, teamwork is critical to the final outcome's quality, but no less to staying within timetables. As a managing partner, I need to recruit and retain the best professionals in the field. Reading this book provided me with new insights and broader perceptions and offered many tips for improving the relationships among employees, team units, external consultants used by our clients, and even with my own business partner. I warmly recommend the book to all owners of small to medium size businesses, particularly if they do not have the resources to hire ongoing consultancy."
Adriana Dvir, architect, Dvir Yehiam Architects and Urban Planners

*

"I gained practical tools for improving outputs by improving synergy with and among employees and clients. **I intend to study this more deeply and apply it in our organization.**"
Chaim Glancer, Engineer & CEO of the Institute of Assessors

CONTENTS

CHAPTER 3 -
How to successfully embed the synergy process 92

CHAPTER 4 - Synergy or Wasted Energy:
Rules and tips for improving interactions 117

BONUS ARTICLE -

INTRODUCTION
Organizational Synergy from a bird's eye view

If developing your organization and maintaining its leading status are important to you, and you want to ensure that your organization operates on the basis of quality interactions in general, and synergistic interactions specifically, then this book is right for you.

How can organizational synergy help your organization? By promoting improved organizational outputs, optimizing mergers or acquisitions, successfully assimilating new and innovative technologies, and developing a range of products and services with relative ease. Simultaneously, you'll see levels of motivation and gratification among employees increase, and the sense of belonging and connection between managers and employees to their workplace will strengthen.

Synergy occurs when diversity exists, but interpersonal differences deter us from opening up to one another. Our tendency to prefer working with people who are similar to ourselves is one of the reasons that synergy is so hard to create.

This book presents a unique perception and method based on a platform of concepts which define it; a model delineating seven forms of interactions; and work tools that allow examining and improving the connection between the organization's diverse forces and resources. You'll find explanations, graphs, examples, a questionnaire for mapping forms of interaction, and pages where you can practice the method. My hope is that taken together, these tools will help you learn the method and acquire the skills that will help you avoid negative interactive forms while reinforcing positive ones, as you take the steps towards your ultimate goal: assimilating synergy in your organization.

Who is this book for?

This book is for you if:

- You're an owner, member of the board, partner or manager in any organization, large or small, in any sector, and you want to improve your organization's outputs by improving its interactions and creating synergy among the organization's employees and units in general, and among board members in particular.
- You're a task force manager, or manage the organization's quality assurance or improvement team, and you wish to improve the team's cohesiveness.
- You're in the human resources, organizational development, or training department field and you're interested in exploring new methods which bring value to the organization.
- You're a lecturer, consultant or student in the field of organizational development, and want to add a model and work tools which have been adapted to the needs of 21st century organizational consultancy.

As with any language, the language of synergy needs to be taught, learned, and practiced. This is why I recommend that you become the first one to practice it while reading this book: in other words, read this book with your pen at hand for entering remarks, because this is definitely a book meant for study. Jot down notes in the margins, underline key points, use colored markers. Do whatever works for you. You'll find that this makes practicing the language of synergy much easier when you reread the sections and come across the notes of significance for you and your organization, and the change it is experiencing.

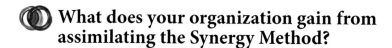 What does your organization gain from assimilating the Synergy Method?

The Synergy Method is a concept I developed **to help managers improve interactions in their organizations.** Improved interactions lead to improved organizational outputs. The method promotes quality interactions among the organization's diverse employees, teams, managers, units and cultures, and **operates at three levels: the individual, the unit, and the organization.**

Working with the synergy approach enables you to **reduce destructive interactions and reinforce productive ones; avoid conflicts; lessen energy wastage; preserve clients and employees; complete the development of new products faster; and primarily, improve organization output as measured by employee morale and gratification, and by the "bottom line" index of profits.**

Adopting the synergistic concept does, however, require change, and any process of change may be perceived by some employees as contrary to their personal interests. A vision for creating a new reality is necessary, as well as commitment on your part to work towards successful synergy assimilation.

How can you get the most out of this book?

The book provides you with background about the Synergy Method and its advantages, and walks you through implementing concrete and essential changes in your organization. This is why I strongly recommend reading the book cover to cover first, marking points you want to reread as you go.

Following the steps involved in a real-time process of change in the organization as closely as possible, each chapter takes you one stage further:

Chapter 1 explains the **concept and principles** of synergy.

Chapter 2 delves deeper into understanding the concept's components, **presents the 7 Forms of Interaction** Model, and provides the **diagnostic questionnaire** which maps interactions in the organization and helps you pinpoint which forms need reinforcement, and which require reduction, in your organization's reality.

Chapter 3 deals with the principles for successfully **assimilating synergy,** and offers a detailed description of the **work process** for implementing the required change.

Chapter 4 reviews the rules and **provides tips**, and many examples, to assist you in leading changes, strengthening the organizational structure, improving work processes, and motivating your employees to the highest level possible.

Throughout the book you'll find **lined pages** where you can pencil in any remarks which reflect the reality you're coping with in your organization. **I encourage you to write down as many remarks and ideas** as you can while reading the book. From experience, **doing so will help you turn the book's knowledge into a useful and beneficial work tool.**

But it's not enough just to read: your success depends on your ability to implement the process by making it relevant to your organization's circumstances and environment. To achieve this, I recommend that you learn the model well, together with the processes described in the book, and tweak them to your organizational reality. Then, examine what works for you, train your employees and managers to use the Synergy Method and the presented processes, and most of all, be persistent with the method, learn from mistakes, correct them and improve.

What is Organizational Synergy?

Synergy is defined as effective cooperation: an activity collaborated on by two or more parties where the result is greater or better than the sum of the results of any single party acting alone. Aristotle is attributed with the statement that "The whole is greater than the sum of its parts" which does a good job of summarizing the concept of synergy.

Synergy can be presented as an amazing formula: $1 + 1 = 3$

This book deals with a unique type of synergy: organizational synergy. To me, the following definition explains its nature clearly: **Organizational synergy is the way interactions occur within an organization or between different organizations which allows creating a new reality by several partners, where one party is unable** (or finds it too difficult) to create that same reality alone **due to economic or other considerations**.

☑ Please note that when I use the term "partners," I'm not necessarily referring to an organization's joint proprietors but to any type of activity that involves two or more entities.

Seven forms of interaction can be found in organizations, and these will be expanded on in Chapter 2. But by way of example, let's look at a merger between two insurance companies. Prior to the merger, each agency specialized in different products and services geared to the market sector each one served. The merger results in a One Stop Shop insurance company for private and commercial clients. The new reality means that clients can find a broader range of insurance needs covered under one roof. For the new organization, the new reality means accessing a larger data base of clients, and an increase in profits far beyond what both organizations could have achieved separately.

Another example would be the natural synergy that human existence is based on, when a man and woman unite for the purpose of establishing a family and bringing children into the world. This example demonstrates the need of both parties to create a new reality while simultaneously coping with the challenges of intensive dialogue which involves two different languages (male and female).

An area in which the significance of organizational synergy manifests clearly is that of customer service. Many organizations operate under the slogan of "the customer is always right," but can't seem to implement this in the field. In many cases issues arise, complaints may be submitted, and a review is conducted to check who is "right". But in truth it makes no difference who is right: the customer will still feel a sense of invasion following the investigation, and the service will be experienced as "not good". The invasive form is one we'll discuss in greater detail later in the book. Quality customer service must be based on creating synergy with the client or, in other words, amping up the phrase "better safe than sorry" to match the needs of customer service. We could paraphrase with "it's better to be smart than right" if we want to promote the "feel good" sensation in our customers.

Case Study

Some years ago I flew with JAL, the Japanese airline. The flight was long and I passed the time reading on-board magazines. One contained an article I found particularly fascinating, about management in Japan. Wanting to continue reading the article, I asked one of the flight crew for permission to take the magazine with me. She answered that it was not really permitted to remove material from the plane. When I explained that the article's content was my field, interested me deeply, and that the magazine was already a month old and a newer publication would likely replace it quite soon, the flight attendant bowed and handed me the magazine, adding "With compliments from Japan Airlines."

Her action showed how the airline trained its staff to make smart decisions and flex boundaries or rules when possible, with

> the aim of providing excellent service. Even though the flight attendant was not among the higher ranking members of an airline's employees, she found the way to synergistically connect with the customer and ensure that I go away with a quality service experience. In chapter 1 we discuss the three types of boundaries at length.

Synergy allows leaving behind the "either / or" mindset, often translated as "it's us or them" typical of western culture, and shifting to inclusive thinking expressed as "both this and that", typical of various eastern cultures. **Synergy is the art of merging opposites, bridging between the need to preserve and the need to change.** Based as it is on an approach of "expanding the options," or as I like to describe it, "having your cake and eating it/"

In game theory terms, synergy is an example of a game that is **not** "zero sum," where one party's profit is balanced by the other party's loss so that the sum total of both evens out to zero. **On the contrary: synergistic thinking allows the organization to simultaneously conduct processes which, in retrospect, seem to be contradictory. These include centralization and decentralization, integration and differentiation, quality improvement and price reduction, and more. These will be discussed in more detail in Chapter 4, under "Tools and processes for reinforcing the creation of synergy."**

The art of merging opposites makes it possible to stay close to an organization's core values while setting more venturesome targets such as simultaneous preservation and change. In Good to Great: *Why Some Companies Make the Leap… And Others Don't*, James Collins and Timothy Judge (define the simultaneity which enhances good outcomes into excellent ones as "Level II Thinking."

Organizational synergy can be implemented in two possible dimensions:
- **The dimension of containment or enabling;** or
- **The dimension of coercion and enforcement.**

1.   In the dimension of containment, or enabling, organizational synergy is carried out through 3 tools: a. inclusion of the diverse; b. practicing how to make boundaries more flexible through openness, attentiveness, empathy or overriding ego; c. improving communication. All of these will be discussed in the book.

Throughout the book, you'll come across the term "ego." According to Freud, ego is the structure that constitutes the primary consciousness in humans. However, I use it more in its slang sense of a highly self-focused individual keen to ensure her or his benefit first and foremost: an egocentric person. Clarifying further, this book uses "ego" to indicate any action an individual takes to glorify her or his own political power within the organization, often at the expense of others.

An example of containment or enabling might be where the board decides to improve synergy among its members. It can choose various methods, such as making each board member more familiar with each other's personal and professional world, conducting a shared leisure activity, and so on.

2. In the dimension of coercion or enforcement, organizational synergy encourages cooperation based on the belief, and in harsher scenarios, the threat, that it is better to cooperate with another person, or a process, even if that person is different from me and I find it difficult to contain him. Often coerced cooperation is the response to a reason such as "no chemistry", or fear of the process.

The most common example of this dimension occurs in mergers and acquisitions. Numerous employees will find themselves in a situation where they have to cooperate and create a new reality even if they cannot contain the other, and perceive the other as a threat. In other words, the thinking is: I'm cooperating with you to create a new reality even though there's no chemistry between us, and perhaps I feel threatened by you, and find it hard to contain your behavior... but I'm cooperating because I believe this approach will be useful.

In the process of assimilating the synergy method described in this book, I have related primarily to the first dimension, because this is the correct dimension for authentic synergistic activity. The second dimension may be used, however, in the short term until the managerial culture is changed, and the organization becomes inclusive, containing, learning and enabling.

Chaordic Organizations is a recently coined term used to describe organizations where order and chaos coexist despite the polarity between them. Just as seemingly polar states coexist in nature, such as day / night, heat / cold, and hunter / prey, such organizations can maintain their balance despite a shift from competition to cooperation among organizations, including between competitors, and cooperation with the environment, including ecology.

Spiritual or esoteric approaches from various religions and beliefs teach us about a power that unifies oppositional forces, a divine entity that is of a higher level than nature. Similarly, the synergy approach allows contrasting forces to unify at the organizational level, despite the difficulty in implementing the method, which itself derives from human nature's tendency to encourage competition and to function according to political or ego-based considerations.

The concept of synergy in the organization developed in parallel with other post-modern approaches, among them shared leadership and collective wisdom, which also stress the premise that the group is always smarter than the individuals comprising it. These approaches focus on improving interactions among the components of the group, and not necessarily on improving the components themselves.

◎ The Paradox of Synergy: If it's so good to work synergistically, why is it so tough to implement?

A synergistic entity is, as we've defined, a new creation, the formation of something that had not existed previously. As we will see in chapter 2, synergy is created only when boundaries are flexible, and communication is very good (we shall call it fusion). Unfortunately very often our tendency is to preserve the existing state and rigidify the boundaries if something threatens it, especially if the threat is beyond our full control or is forced on us, such as employee dismissals or mergers. The communication in these situations tends to be political, and even violent.

In other words, if I receive a surprise message that the organization has been purchased by another or is about to be merged with another, and I now need to work synergistically with people I don't know, and even be forced to work with people who were previously marked as "the competition," I may feel very threatened, no matter whether I hold a senior or junior position.

Questions surface at the personal level: Will I still work in the organization once the process has been completed? Will I have the same status? And if so, will I now be subordinate to a new authority? Before the merger I answered direct to the CEO, so will I be subordinate to a lower rank now? and so forth.

Employees in the organization know that these kinds of questions remain open even if addressed at some level at the outset of the process. After all, no one knows what the final outcome could be when such a major change is instituted.

Every change occurring in an organization threatens the existing order, even if the change is no more than the temporary appointment of a team leader.

Synergistic conduct in most cases means committing to stepping outside the comfort zone, which inherently arouses anything from mild to strong resistance. In such a reality our natural tendency is to rigidify our boundaries, dig down into our stances, and give preference to personal interests rather than those of our unit or the organization. This is where personality traits also come into play, such as a tendency to conservatism, anxiety, or ego driven choices. Individuals with these traits will tend to cooperate less and find it harder to be flexible or connect to the quality of communication needed to create synergy. More on this in Chapter 2.

Synergy, then, means we need to commit to softening our boundaries, breaking through the organizational structure, and using all possible resources. The solution to the challenge and its issues lies in shaping a stimulating vision for all the organization's members. The leader, even if in a relatively low ranking role, must show fellow team workers that the new status is not threatening to each team member's interests but actually preserves and protects them.

For example, if a particular organization is on the verge of collapse and is acquired by another, the purchase ensures that employees of the first will still have a workplace. Some may indeed benefit from promotion, or be offered a new role. If employees believe possibilities exist for them, they will be more open to putting their personal interests aside and examining the new options from a different perspective. They will also be more willing to accept the price of the transitional stage because they understand that it embodies the possibility of a better future.

Even when leadership and vision exist, they aren't enough to make achieving integration simple. The organization must be patient, and willing to invest a good deal of energy in handling conflicts that will surely arise. The organization must tirelessly market the concept of change to its employees, stressing its usefulness. This doesn't mean that all aspects of the situation should be presented through rose-tinted glasses; they should be discussed as they realistically stand while emphasizing the various advantages it may bring.

One way to overcome the difficulty of creating synergy at the individual level is to try and enjoy the process itself. Outputs and objectives are very important, but if we experience the process as enjoyable, it will be so much simpler to reach those objectives. I recommend reading the work of Dr. Tal Ben-Shahar, which you'll find listed in the References at the end of this book.

The paradox of synergy is one of the best reasons for involving a professional consultant that will assist the organization's leader in marketing and implementing change in the organization. From my experience, in cases where I managed to create synergy with the CEO or a senior manager, this success radiated out, influenced employees and allowed us to embed the process far more smoothly.

What led me to working with synergy, and why was this book written?

Right before you jump into the deep end, let me share a personal anecdote from the earliest days of my involvement with the field of human interactions and which eventually led to writing this book.

In 1982, I took a long vacation from my job, planning to leverage this time for writing my doctoral dissertation, which dealt with the management of independent operative units in organizations. (For the article, scan the QR on the back cover of the book) At the time, this was a very new field. And at the time, I had no idea that my dissertation would become my professional career as an organizational consultant, and open doors to specializing in relationships and interactions.

As part of the doctoral studies, I conducted comprehensive research in three organizations which were very different from each other, but shared one common denominator: each was about to assimilate organization-wide changes including in its independent operational units. The organizations were: a business concern, which transitioned to managing its production plants as autonomous profit centers; the IDF (Israel Defense Forces), where interactions and management norms between the human resources division and the various military wings were being examined as a result of changes to the remuneration framework for non-commissioned officers ; and the Amal education network, which was examining reciprocity between its schools and the network's administration during a period where broader powers had been assigned to school principals.

Despite the blatant differences among these organizations, and perhaps because of them, I learned of the important place that interactions hold in organizations, especially as far as relations between headquarters and the field units, as well as the difficulty in promoting and maintaining a system of quality relationships, let alone synergistic interactions, in the organization.

In 1996 I started work as an organizational consultant in the Israel branch of the social enterprise known as Hadassah Women's Organization. At the time, two culturally different volunteer groups could be identified in the organization. One comprised English speaking women who had immigrated to Israel from the USA, and who sought to continue their activities in the organization, especially in the area of fundraising. The second group primarily comprised

Hebrew speaking women, Israeli volunteers who wished to contribute to the community and be involved in the field.

One of the difficulties experienced by the organization's management at the time was in creating a link between these two groups with their diverse cultures. The organization clearly needed a good dosage of synergy to help them bridge and resolve the intercultural conflicts, and allow productive outcomes.

Wanting to bring the organization into a synergistic state, we conducted an intensive process at three levels:

- Volunteers: we ran workshops in each geographic location, to members of both cultures;
- Group leaders and management: we held a synergy course, which dealt with spreading and preserving the synergy method in the organization;
- National administration: we took actions to improve the work processes and strengthen the atmosphere of synergy which had been created.

This process of consultancy served as the basis for developing my **7 Forms of Interaction Model**, which is at the core of the Synergy Method. You'll find the 7F Model presented in Chapter 2.

Since then, I have developed the synergy assimilation method through two parallel avenues, which also interact synergistically: a. consulting for dozens of projects, from small to massive, in diverse sectors; b. developing the synergy method and work tools to support its assimilation in the organization. I have personally experienced the transition from an organizational culture that places emphasis on an individual's specialization (talents) as the factor for success, to an organizational culture typified by synergistic cooperation and the creation of a reality that, time after time, leads to new achievements.

For the past 20 years or so, I worked with hundreds of students and managers, and dozens of organizations and projects, and too often have I heard statements that admit to a lack of synergy. Here are some of them:

This workplace could be fun if only Dave would...
>   Every workplace has its "Dave". Feel free to replace the name with one that works for you.

I feel like a salaried worker in my own company!
>   That hardly adds to my motivation! Spoken by a proprietor partner in the financial sector.

I don't know where the fine line is between my role and Emma's. No matter how often you explain it, Jack's not getting the job done the way it should be. I end up having to do the work myself.
>   This comes from an industrial concern's VP, who invaded the role of one of the manufacturing plant managers.

I leave Julie messages, but the *$#@! doesn't get back to me!
>   Okay, let's admit it: this happens in every organization.

Handling this client somehow falls between the cracks.
>   This is from a sales team in an industrial plant purchased by another firm. Obviously the merger between the two sales systems did not succeed.

The sales team just does not understand our limitations.
>   So said the production manager in a company producing microwaves.

The IT team invents software that just causes even more pressure.
>   This is something I've heard from clients and employees in numerous organizations which experienced the sense of invasion and lack of synergy between the information systems deployed in the organization and the systems' real time users.

Tip: Write down some of the remarks you have heard or hear from your employees, managers, or work colleagues in your organization. What would you tell me, if I had asked to interview you? Just write down whatever you think is appropriate at this point in time. You can always repeat this exercise at later stages. After you finish the book, I recommend that you reread these statements.

_____

_____

_____

_____

_____

_____

_____

By contrast, when my work with the organization reaches its end and the process or workshops I have held are complete, I hear different statements. One of the typical remarks was made by Yoram Shifer, joint CEO of Ziv, Shifer & Co., a CPA office that I assisted as they conducted a merger:

"Working with you helped us understand the destructive forms of action we had been working under, and redirect the energies of the merged company's partners and employees towards creating organizational synergy. Thanks to you, the cooperation between the two offices and the two organizational cultures improved, matched by improved profits."

Over time, I realized that learning the forms of interaction really does help improve the organization. That is when I decided to share my knowledge with as many managers and consultants as I possibly could. My decision was reinforced in 2011 when I was set for a routine surgical procedure that led to complications, and left me spending most of my time until the end of 2013 in and out of hospitals, undergoing repeat or corrective surgical procedures, and frequently hanging between life and death.

These events led me to take several significant decisions about my life. The first: not only was surrendering to my medical situation not an option, but I would overcome it, get healthy, and continue contributing to the community in the best way I know how: with my skills and capabilities. The second: I could fulfill the decision to keep contributing by writing this book.

I wish you a pleasant and productive read, and the chance to create a new reality for your organization.

CHAPTER 1
How to achieve more: Diving into the concept of synergy

Reading this chapter will familiarize you with the background to synergy as a concept by understanding the historical context that led to its development, and the basic elements it comprises: diversity, boundaries and communication.

At the end of the chapter, you will find several pages where you can record remarks relative to the organizational reality in which you function. Recording your thoughts will help you turn the knowledge you gain into information relevant to your needs.

The twentieth century was a period of social and economic upheavals. These, naturally influenced the organizational structures of companies and businesses. The early twentieth century was typified by the development of modern business, industrial and governmental organizations. All were structured around specialization and very clear work procedures, defined as scientific management.

The principle behind the organization was the assembly line, where employees worked and were overseen by the work manager, usually someone with professional skills who had slightly more experience. There was no large professional division; the manager, now replaced by CEO, was usually the owner of the business. Unlike the current organizational structures, there were almost no additional departments subordinate or parallel to the manager. There would be no R&D department, training department, and definitely no human resources department. Processes were understood, clear, and employment of experts only occurred in response to a problem or a specific issue in the organization.

Charlie Chaplin, in his film "Modern Times," illustrated just how deeply the sense of alienation and mechanical functioning controlled every manufacturing plant or organization in the early 1900s. As the years passed and post-modernism increasingly spread, organizations became more professional. Many emphasized quality, team work, and cooperation among employees. Towards the twentieth century's close, we increasingly encounter organizations and manufacturing plants of the kind familiar to us now. The fixed and unchanging assumptions were abandoned, and post-modern perceptions adopted instead.

Most of the highly successful organizations of the twenty-first century in all areas of industry, production and services are post-modern and devote significant resources to developing the organizational structure, increasing its human capital, and promoting synergy among employees and among the organization's units. By contrast, organizations which did not assimilate the changes or adapt their organizational processes in line with social and economic changes that are occurring worldwide, find it tough to keep ahead of competition in the business sector and to address consumer demands.

One important characteristic of post-modern organizations is the transition from working with experts to teamwork. We've become accustomed to believing that solutions will come from smart people. An article on collective intelligence, published by Woolley, et al, (listed in the references) in the 2010 Science magazine, sheds light on how it is precisely this ability to work together that becomes the basis for an organization's success in both the business and private sectors. This has clearly manifested in the changes to threshold requirements organizations apply when recruiting employees, whether at senior or lower levels. In the past, the senior stratum of an organization's functionaries had to be experts in their fields: for example, a human resources manager needed to hold specialized knowledge in the field of human resources, and filling the role required providing management with current professional information relative to establishing and operating the organization's human resources system.

Similarly, the vice president of operations had to possess professional knowledge in the sphere of industrial engineering and management or mechanical engineering; and the role additionally required being fully fluent with the field and providing the organization with specific information when called on to present it in board meetings. Organizations were structured around specialized departments and work processes rarely crossed from one department to another.

At the close of the 20th century and start of the 21st century, differentiated domains are found with decreasing frequency. Many organizations have adopted the teamwork structure at all organizational levels, from work teams to board meetings, and to special improvement teams whose members come from different departments. This is especially true of organizations seeking to assimilate methodologies such as slim-line management, TQM (Total Quality Management) and others.

Board members are also required to be fluent in areas of knowledge held by other board members, at least at the basic level, towards ensuring they can discuss issues with each other and solve problems synergistically. In other words, post-modern organizations will frequently aspire to achieve integration within the organization and cooperation among all units and departments, and the HQ's work will not only be conducted through board meetings but at all levels of the organization, and in coordination with the various levels.

All the above is relevant to small businesses, too: specialized companies such as law offices, accounting firms, engineering contractors, insurance agencies, startups, tourism offices, light industry and more. These businesses, where the absence of a HQ is normal, need synergy among the partners, particularly in light of the wave of mergers and acquisitions typical of the outset of this century.

I have no doubt that in light of real time actions, 21st century organizations will need to be more synergistic than those of the previous century. This trend seems set to continue in the future.

 Fundamental concepts in synergy: Diversity, boundaries and communication

Interactions in general and synergistic interactions in particular, are based on three fundamental concepts: diversity, boundaries, and communication. Diversity is vital for creating synergy, while boundaries and communication are the two axes that generally serve to define forms of interaction and forms of synergistic interaction in particular.

Read more on the various forms in Chapter 2.

 Diversity

Diversity is the vital basis for creating synergy: synergy cannot be created between identical components. As I noted in the introduction, the most basic form of synergy is that created when a man and a woman decide to establish a family and bring children into the world. This complex process manifests through gender difference. Diversity is not only vital for establishing the family but introduces a new area of consideration: how to shape synergy in the new reality.

Let me demonstrate with a personal story that links gender diversity and cultural diversity.

Case Study

At 21 years old, I was ready for a change of pace. I took off for Austria, where I studied sketching for a brief period. There I met a young woman who later became my partner. It was a wonderful, romantic relationship: here were a young man and a young woman in love, in their youthful years.

We were very aware of the differences between us. I was Jewish, and Israeli. She was Christian, and Austrian. With our youthful innocence we believed that love conquers all or, in the language of synergy which I use these days, we had a vision, we thought we'd succeed in creating synergy and with it, a new reality. But when we tried to function in Israel's reality, countless difficulties surfaced: religious conversion, employment, and cultural adaption. At some point we threw our hands up into the air: we gave up, realizing that the differences had won and the synergistic process had failed.

I am not sure to what degree this personal experience led me to delving into otherness and diversity, but it definitely proves just how difficult it is to forge intercultural links.

I imagine a large number of readers are familiar with versions of this incident. We are naturally curious about discovering new cultures and places. We love traveling abroad to visit other countries, but even then some of us try to live as though we're back home, preferring to use our mother tongues in the hotel with other tourists from our home country, watch TV channels in our home tongue if possible, and eat familiar foods, as evidenced by the branches of fast food chains full of tourists familiar with their products from "back home."

We naturally tend to evaluate and compare our status to that of others, checking how similar or different we are from people in our surroundings. We seem to have a need to notice the differences, to select and categorize, as part of our basic need for survival and self-protection. Simply put, anyone who's different from me doesn't belong to my group, is not part of my tribe, and therefore could be a threat to me and require me to protect myself. But the more we allow curiosity to lead us forward, the more we learn to contain, respect and even understand the other. We can adopt more flexible boundaries, as this book will teach. And doing so is a necessary condition for creating synergy.

It may be that my personal experience and effort in linking two diverse elements caused me to subconsciously work in synergy. I understood that an exciting vision, good intentions and confident declarations just aren't enough. I also realized that all the managers of companies and organizations talking about wanting to create synergy, buy out companies, or make significant changes, do not produce quality synergy. And that's because the managers aren't aware of the characteristics which differentiate people, whether at intra- or inter-organizational levels.

Many managers view employees as part of the organization's property, as evident by the term "human capital," and therefore pay little attention to the diversity among employees. As expressed in the past by one of my clients: "Forget about that psychology of yours! Employees come to their jobs in order to work, so don't start with 'their different needs'..." Happily, that old fashioned approach is fast fading, and certainly won't be found in post-modern organizations which seek to advance, develop and succeed, nor in organizations wishing to embed synergy.

I want to emphasize that diversity within the concept of synergy does not imply inequality, but relates to dissimilarity or non-uniformity. If we examine diversity between men and women in organizations, we find that it manifests in the managerial style of men and women in leadership roles. Many organizations have come to acknowledge and respect this diversity. The Bank of Scotland, for example, is diligent about reserving several slots for women on their Board of Directors, not as an outcome of regulations but due to the insight that diversity improves the Directorate's decision making processes. **This is synergy.**

In other words, despite board members' diverse managerial styles, the contribution of each, whether male or female, may be of equal value. The views held by men and women board members are of great value to the organization, and salaries of these managers should accordingly be at the same level. Perhaps this seems a simplistic if not banal example, but it demonstrates very clearly how diversity does not assume inequality.

Diversity manifests through characteristics which differentiate individuals, whether that diversity is based on knowledge, role or profession; on cultural or social customs or experiences; or inherent traits such as gender, age, race, or origin. In many countries, legislation prohibits discrimination on the basis of such diversity.

The concept of diversity in the perception of synergy is supported by two additional concepts: **uniformity**, and **uniqueness**, both of which complete the implementation of diversity in the organization. Organizations which allow these concepts to manifest are promoting their organizational synergy. In general, the concept of uniformity expresses itself in the definition of shared direction, purpose and vision, while uniqueness expresses itself in providing legitimacy and encouraging the organization's departments and units to develop their own organizational sub-culture, a move which suits complex organizations.

You'll find an in-depth discussion of these concepts in the bonus article on page 175.

Boundaries

Synergistic perception views boundaries as a means of tangibly expressing diversity among employees or units in the organization. Boundaries are generally in place to protect us, based on the idea that the more diverse we are, the more vulnerable we are and in need of protection. Boundaries and limitations are intricately linked: on one hand, fixing boundaries protects the individual or entity; on the other hand, boundaries simultaneously set limitations on any individual's or entity's relationship with any other.

According to the synergy approach, it's not always necessary to "break through boundaries," an action which can be seen as invasive by others. Instead, boundaries can be flexed, enabling interaction between diverse factors within those boundaries.

Boundaries are where interactions naturally occur. For example, let's take boundaries between countries: the more that a country's citizens or, as some may say, that country's leaders, feel different from the citizens of a neighboring country, the more need they'll have of protecting themselves with rigid borders. In Israel we feel this particularly strongly, which gives rise to a need for strong, clearly delineated borders, such as fences and walls separating us from neighboring nations.

In the organizational reality, boundaries and diversity may manifest in the objectives set by the organization, a department or a unit, or personal objectives of employees. A very important objective for a production manager, for example, is long production runs, as a way of reducing the cost of the scheduled dead times needed for machinery maintenance or production adaptations. The primary objective of a marketing manager will be to match the product as closely as possible to consumer needs, which actually requires small production runs. The objective of the organization, to produce profits, depends on both.

Boundaries and diversity may manifest in additional areas:

◐Employee levels of expertise and experience: diversity in professions and specializations, the types of organizations or organizational environments they experienced in previous jobs, and so on.

◐The degree of responsibility and authority: what the

employee is responsible for, and what powers have been delegated to empower the responsibility.

⦿Organizational hierarchic structure: these are status indicators applied by the organization to express intra-organizational boundaries. But the more we want to reinforce synergy in the organization, the more we need to forego these statuses. Military organizations, for example, place strong emphasis on hierarchic status and its symbols, such as rank, use of different dining halls for commanders, allocation of different classes of vehicles for officers, and so on. Hierarchic manifestations of this nature make it harder to assimilate the language of synergy.

⦿Organizational culture: boundaries and diversity may manifest in organizational culture. Every organization operating in the global reality has both a global organizational culture, and a local culture derived from the fact that its activities are based in a specific country, company or market place. Within the organization itself, diverse cultures may exist alongside each other: the culture of office employees may be different from that of employees working in the field, or the culture of employees in the R&D department may be different from that of sales staff, production staff or the marketing unit.

But from an overall perspective, we want each unit in the organization to have its own culture, because we want R&D staff to have flexible creative thinking, and so might be less strict with them on maintaining timetables or budgets. By contrast, the production unit should be characterized by precision; keeping to schedules is hugely important.

Creating synergy often requires us to find that golden path between the need to protect diversity in the organization, and the need to flex the boundaries between those very elements of diversity.

⦿Physical and territorial boundaries: physical boundaries may manifest in multinational organizations which operate across several countries, or even in an organization run out of a specific country but having numerous international branches. Examples are banks, insurance companies, or large corporations with manufacturing plants in different geographic locations.

Case study

Some years ago I taught at Assumption University in Thailand. One group of students executed its final project in a Thai cable TV company. The company's expansion meant that its existing physical space no longer matched its needs, a problem it solved by renting additional offices in another building, which was physically distant from the company's center of activities. This separation between departments constituted a physical boundary, which led to difficulty in the HQ's work, compared to the previous situation where all activities took place under the same physical roof.

Most organizations don't give much thought to this situation in advance, and only in retrospect find that they need to structure mechanisms and technological systems that allow making the boundaries more flexible to overcome barriers.

What has the strongest impact on an organization's boundaries and diversity?

Ego.

The greater the platform given to ego among employees in an organization, which makes boundaries between them more rigid, the harder it becomes to attain synergy. A spiral link exists between flexing boundaries, and taking actions based on a group or cooperational mindset. The safer an employee feels within her or his boundaries, and the better the quality of communication, the more comfortable that same employee will feel about working in a team and foregoing ego based actions.

Case study

Not so long ago I had a conversation with the manager of a large organization's computing unit. She described the difficulties and problems working with her subordinates, the project managers. She claimed that issues of ego primarily typified male employees. Whether they are senior managers, or professionals such as technicians or project managers, they found it hard to "forego their egos," which made it harder to institute processes of synergy in the organization. That, in turn, caused the failure of attempts to develop synergistic dialogue. The manager described two primary manifestations of this situation: the attitude of the project managers, all of whom were male, towards her as a female manager; and the way these project managers functioned relative to the projects' internal clients served by these projects.

A person's perceptions of her or his ego, self-image and status in the company or organization are based on personal traits, needs, wishes, fears and aspirations, all of which may cause rigidity in the boundaries between that person and others in the shared environment, and bring about the failure of any attempt at creating cooperation and synergy.

Opposition to cooperation doesn't only derive from ego, however, but also from a lack of confidence, from rigidity, levels of internalization, difficulty in adapting to change and leaving the comfort zone, and additional personality traits. And of course the combination alters from one person to another.

Now that we've reviewed the various ways that diversity and boundaries are expressed, it's important to note and categorize the types of boundaries that synergistic perceptions relate to, and to understand the components of synergy better by diving deep into the language of synergy.

The language of synergy relates to **three types of boundaries**:

- ◎ Rigid
- ◎ Flexible
- ◎ Blurred

◎ Rigid boundaries

Rigidity describes boundaries that are difficult to overcome or cross. They often exist because of a sense of threat or fear, depending on each circumstance's unique reasons. In any event, when a person, team, department, organization or even nation sets up rigid boundaries, that entity invests effort in making them hard to cross.

An example is the cold war between eastern and western European countries, where borders were extremely rigid. Anyone living in Berlin, Germany's capital, could clearly see where that rigid physical boundary was by looking at the wall that split the city. Even before the wall, it was very difficult to move from one side of the city to the other.

◐ Flexible boundaries

Flexible boundaries occur when both parties on either side of the boundary make an effort to recalibrate boundaries as "lightweight." Looking at European borders again, these days they are far more flexible, especially if both countries are members of the European Union.

The EU, established for the purpose of creating a new and stronger synergy from countries pooled together rather than operating as single components, sought to cope better with other countries in the global village that is now part of our lives. But to create this synergy, it was necessary to soften the borders between countries both at the physical and economic levels. For the former, border crossings between countries were made more flexible, and the need for country-specific passports was cancelled. For the latter, a shared currency was issued, the Euro, which replaced country-specific currencies in almost all member nations. But as the trend in recent years shows, when economic and personal safety concerns increase, the otherness among member countries, such as the otherness between Greece or Spain and Germany, makes it harder for diversity to find its synergy, and demands to disband the EU are increasingly being voiced. The United Kingdom is the first country to do so.

◎ Blurred boundaries

These are boundaries with missing parts. An example would be when there is no clear division of roles between an organization's employees. Blurred boundaries prevent creating synergy.

Blurring often comes about as a result of disagreement, rather than any specific intention to rigidify or flex boundaries. An example would be borders which separate nations by limiting cultural flow, while simultaneously bonding them fluidly by serving as free trade zones.

Case study

Some years ago I provided consultancy to a company producing raw materials for sanitation products. During that period, the company encountered new markets in Eastern European countries for the first time. These countries previously had not held any trade relations with Israel.

The number of marketing and sales staff was equivalent to the number of active markets: one for the American market, one for the western European market, and one for the Asian market. The distinction between them, being geographical region, was very clear but the organizational culture and climate of interactions made flexibility and creative solutions possible.

As chance would have it, just as the markets were opening up in Eastern Europe, a major trade fair was held in Germany and a decision needed to be taken about which of the marketing and sales representatives would take on the role of handling East Europe. The immediate back-stop solution would have been to choose one of the marketing and sales staff who spoke Russian. But in the long term, the company needed to find a far more institutionalized way of addressing this situation.

The good relations among the sales team made it possible to flex boundaries and find a creative situation-specific solution. But had they operated from stances of ego and interpersonal competition, as often happens among sales managers, there would be a far greater likelihood that finding a solution would have failed.

Why do blurred boundaries exist?

What causes an organization's boundaries to blur? Any number of reasons comes to mind. The most trivial is that some of characteristics of that boundary, such as definition of role, areas of responsibility, or delegation of power, are missing or aren't sufficiently clarified. Another reason is that ongoing changes occur, making it harder to keep the boundaries stable.

It is frequently said these days that the only stable, constant aspect of current organizations is change! Many organizations cope with what seems like constant and fast paced change: new markets open up, new products are being launched into the market, and many organizations carry out acquisitions or mergers that lead to broad, significant change. Frequent changes to boundaries leads to obscurity. Hazy boundaries arouse conflict when disagreement exists.

An employee who experienced change in the organization may come to the realization that there is no other choice, and will therefore accept the new boundaries, but may still feel insecure about the organization's goals or the targets that the organization may now require. This feeling may give rise to another: that lines have been blurred or territories invaded. We'll discuss this more in the next chapter.

An example would be the merger of two pharmaceutical companies. Further to the merger, all the sales staff are required to sell products unfamiliar to them. Organization managers need to take into account that the learning process takes time, and usually a lot more time than what has been allocated to the process. This kind of situation can cause problems when dealing with clients, and cause a sense of obscurity or even invasion among the sales representatives.

How can we differentiate between flexible boundaries and blurred boundaries?

A predominant trait in the organizations of today is

their flexible boundaries in general, and in defining roles, responsibilities and delegated powers in particular. Managers sometimes call this "blurred boundaries." But according to the synergistic approach, there is no confusion between blurred boundaries, where parts of a boundary's definition are missing, and flexible boundaries, where the definition is clear but the parties involved are comfortable with assisting each other. In other words, flexibility can manifest in the division of work after clear boundaries have been set. I wish to stress that according to the synergistic approach, all the types of boundaries coexist, and the only issue is determining what the balance will be.

This is a good point to stop and remember that defining a boundary's degree of blurring or flexibility is subjective, and every employee will experience these traits differently. One of an organization's purposes when aiming for synergy is to reduce these sensations of blurring among its employees, and clarify boundaries. I'll expand on this in Chapter 4, but for now I'll shed some light on the problematics of the issue, using the following four examples.

 ### Four examples of distinction between flexible boundaries and blurred boundaries

Kyle is the secretary at a legal office with three partners and two interns. Starting out, Kyle was unsure what services should be supplied to whom: does Kyle photocopy material for interns or only for the full partners? Over time, files to be photocopied piled up on Kyle's desk. Raising the issue with one of the partners was answered with statements like "If you have time, do it" or "No need to make an issue of it" and even "It's important to be flexible..." These and other responses did nothing to clarify what was expected of him.

This situation of blurred boundaries led to Kyle's sense of invasion, and conflicts between him and the interns. In a process of boundary definitions, it was clarified that no, Kyle isn't expected to photocopy for interns, but in cases of emergency, and if Kyle is free, it is correct to photocopy for them. Currently, when an intern asks for Kyle's assistance in photocopying material or organizing an urgent file for a client, the decision on whether and how to respond rests entirely with Kyle, who is happy to help in most cases.

In retrospect, there was no more than a small change but if we were to ask Kyle about it, we'd find it was highly significant for him. It legitimized his ability to weigh the issue and respond accordingly, since it was now clear that first and foremost, Kyle was expected to fulfill the tasks that fell clearly into the definition of his role. This demonstrates how blurred boundaries can create conflict in the organization, whereas clear boundaries prevent them.

An additional example in this context can be found in companies just starting out, or in small family companies which are often typified by flexible rather than blurred boundaries. The atmosphere in these organizations is often "everyone does everything" and for as long as all the workers/partners define the boundaries between them as flexible, there's no problem with it. But the moment that any of them feel these boundaries have become too blurred and give rise to conflict, it becomes necessary to clarify them. This is a natural process which often occurs on its own as the company grows.

Defining boundaries does not need to include the totality of tasks an employee is expected to carry out. That degree of definition is difficult to attain in a frequently changing reality, especially in organizations in states of growth but it is important to involve the employee in defining the job's boundaries and allow the employee some room for weighing considerations. This prevents the employee from feeling threatened as a result of experiencing blurred boundaries.

This third example comes from my personal experience: how my failure became a learning curve. In my work as a consultant, I followed through on the merger process between two industrial manufacturers. At the outset of my work, I clarified that a need exists to examine the production processes, and for that purpose I invited a colleague, an industrial management engineer. I thought the boundaries between us were clear, both to ourselves and to management, which was why I felt comfortable raising differences of opinion between us with the client, in this case at a board meeting held to discuss the findings.

I viewed the situation as having flexible boundaries, but the plant's CEO said, "You're Mr. Synergy but there's no synergy between you and the other consultant."

And he was right. I didn't take into account the perception of the plant managers who experienced the dynamic between my colleague and me as blurring rather than as two avenues which required integration.

This example demonstrates just how subjective the distinction between blurring and flexibility really is.

And finally, an example of symbiosis from the animal world: The blue-streak cleaner wrasse is a fish that cleans up food remnants from the jaws of other fish, including fish of prey. There is no blurring of boundaries here. Each fish is clear on its boundaries, and does not forego a single of its traits. However, there is mutuality which allows flexing the boundaries between them, and therefore the creature which preys on other fish allows this one, the wrasse, to enter its territory without preying on it.

Symbiosis, being cooperation for the sake of mutual benefit, is a form of synergy that demonstrates how there is no need for personal chemistry in order to achieve it. Sometimes it's enough just to be willing to forego ego in order to reach an achievement which neither party can attain alone. Working with employees, however, it is worth investing in interpersonal chemistry which will promote **fusing communication**, expanded on in the next section, and making boundaries more flexible.

Calamitous states which may rigidify boundaries

Having clarified the boundary patterns, I will now present states of calamity that may tighten the boundaries within an organization, and turn them from flexible to rigid.

Previously, ego, and personality traits that influence us, such as fear or personal aspirations, were noted as factors in rigidifying boundaries and creating personal territory within the organization. Below are some additional states which may shift flexible or blurred boundaries into rigid boundaries.

◍ Collective agreements with unions which make it harder for an organization to reassign employees, make changes to role definitions, or renegotiate pension terms. All these aspects rigidify boundaries.

◍ Excessive emphasis on personal competition within the organization. An example is a salary structure that encourages personal competition, as is often customary among sales staff or client portfolio managers.

◍ Differences in attitudes between different groups of employees, or worker discrimination, such as calling groups Generation 1 and Generation 2, or fully salaried organizational employees versus sub-contracting workers.

◍ Use of a strict hierarchic structure to rank roles and delegations of power.

◍ Use of external markers of rank.

◍ Lack of cooperation on the part of key functionaries in the organization.

◍ Organizational culture which: promote the use of power and politics in management; punish mistakes; give no room for bottom up feedback etc.

All the above can rigidify boundaries between employees and the organization, or between an organization's various departments.

Communication

The second axis for basing synergy in an organization is that of communication. It allows the organization to conduct interactions among the various persons and assist integration.

Communication patterns according to synergistic perception

Because the field of communication is relatively familiar to managers and organizational consultants, I'll expand on it less. However, in every process of work on interactions in the organization, we relate to **three patterns of communication** occurring between two parties or among employees:

One-way communication pattern. This form of communication occurs when one party conveys a view without giving consideration to the opinion or wishes of the other party, and without coordinating with the other party. One-way communication may manifest in interactions between countries, such as when East Germany halted movement across the porous Cold War border and built a wall that split Berlin overnight, without asking West Germany for agreement, permission or cooperation; nuclear powers faced off against each other at this location, and people trying to escape from East to West were easily picked off by guards on the wall. I am not making any kind of political statement through this example, but merely wish to point out how one-way communication does not contribute to the quality of interaction between the two sides, and definitely does not allow synergy to develop in an organization.

In the organization, fixed procedures, standards and processes are manifestations of one-way communication.

Two-way (mutual) communication patterns
This communication mode is conducted in tandem between two parties, and is therefore sometimes known

as mutual communication. Two-way communication occurs when two countries are negotiating peace agreements, for example, or when signing trade agreements.

Currently most communication in organizations is two-way: the employee approaches superiors, or subordinates, and expects them to respond, which creates a two-way exchange of information between the parties as a way of completing a task.

Direct or face to face two-way communication adds another layer of non-verbal communication through body language, making it of higher quality than email or written correspondence, and even of higher quality than phone calls, which do allow a certain amount of additional communication through tone of voice.

◉ Fusing communication patterns

Fusion is the only type of communication that enables creating synergistic patterns and assimilating synergistic language in the organization. More on this in the next chapter.

Fusing communication is typified by two or more different parties communicating with each other at such high quality that they eventually create a new reality, just as fusion between two materials creates the new, third material.

An example of fusing communication can be found in organizations that unite for the purpose of creating together a more powerful new reality, than either could attain separately. Examples are the USA, the UN or the EU. In business organizations this will manifest in successful mergers, or organizations that established joint subsidiaries for the purpose of promoting a specific project together.

As part of the flexible dimensions of interaction, fusing communication requires high degrees of listening, empathy and acceptance of diversity or the other. Fusion in communication can be developed through various techniques such as non-verbal communication, empathic communication or outreach. However, creating and maintaining the high level of communication which fusion gives rise to, additionally requires relating to issues of law and ethics, and to work processes that constitute the vital conditions for its existence.

The EU, for example, established the European Parliament as a body aimed at allowing the diverse countries to express their needs. This platform serves as a focal point for encounters among diverse ethnic groups, and promotes ongoing development of fusing communication.

A client once told me how he and his partners would take a ski vacation each year. In other words, they created a window of time for shared informal activity beyond the framework of their work, establishing excellent conditions for shaping fusing communication, should the quality of communication resulting from this shared time be of good quality.

In Chapter 4 you'll find extended information on improving communication, and details of some techniques for achieving this.

An important point, in summary: I emphasize that the process of creating synergy must be carried out in a specific order. First, we need to reduce blurred boundaries and manifestations of rigid boundaries. Then we can work on communication.

Organizations which seek to solve work issues and problems of interaction often invest in improving communication among employees, training staff, and structuring trust around experiential activities, or "outdoor training." All such activities are ahead of their time if boundaries have not yet been clearly defined, and agreed on in advance. The correct order is to examine, first, how the various roles in the organization are defined, then reach agreement on those definitions and coordinate expectations. This makes the process of improving communication both more effective and more efficient.

Summary and your personal workbook

In this chapter we looked at the main concepts relating to perceptions of synergy. I suggest that you write down for yourself the main points that came to your mind while reading and, particularly, what's relevant for your organization or unit, and what you'd like to see changed.

Note that if you're in planning or implementational stages of change in the organization, I recommend that you relate to the old situation and not the new one you're seeking to create and still is not fully tangible. In the coming chapters we'll look at the new, desirable status.

Perception of synergy: in your opinion, what is most relevant in the reality of your organization?

_____

_____

_____

Diversity: which manifesting diversities have the most impact on your organization? How do you bring them together?

_____

_____

_____

Boundaries: which boundary patterns are most relevant for your organization?

Add details and examples: Rigid boundaries / Flexible boundaries / Blurred boundaries

_____

_____

_____

_____

Communication: how would you describe the nature of communication in your organization? Is there room for improvement? List the various ways in which communication is conducted in your organization.

_____

_____

_____

_____

One-way communication

_____

_____

_____

_____

Two-way communication

_____

_____

_____

_____

Fusing communication

_____

_____

_____

_____

_____

_____

_____

CHAPTER 2
Synergy perception in depth: 7F Model – the 7 Forms of Interaction Model and Mapping Questionnaire

Chapter 2 aims to assist you in improving interactions and outputs in your organization, through:
◐ **Learning about the 7 Forms of Interaction Model, and mapping them in your organization.**
◐ **Understanding the quality form of synergy and its significance in your workplace by familiarizing with the four principles for creating synergy.**
◐ **Reducing the damage caused by destructive forms of interaction.**
◐ **Exploring and practicing the interaction mapping questionnaire.**
◐ **Comprehending the different aspects of synergy and their significance for you.**

According to the The Synergy Method, 7 forms of interaction occur in every organization and at every point in time, as represented by the following chart.

Later in this chapter you'll find more detailed discussion on how the types of boundaries and communication shape the forms of interaction.

The model shows that these seven forms of interaction are subdivided into three categories or groups of interactions, based on their contribution to the well-being and outputs of the organization: quality interactions, neutral interactions and destructive interactions.

The two circles, in red and blue, represent two partners in the interaction, whether these are employees, units or entire

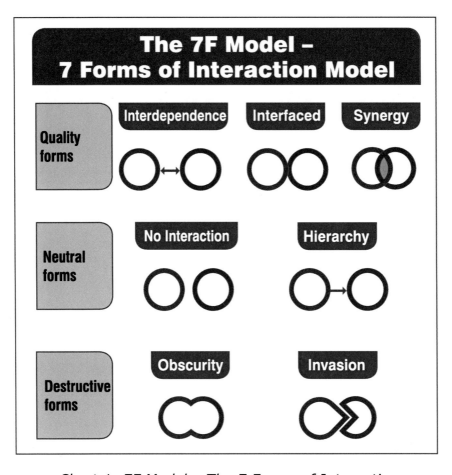

Chart 1: 7F Model – The 7 Forms of Interaction

The 7 Forms of Interaction Model is a graphic representation of the seven interactions that occur in organizations.

Each interaction expresses:

⦾ **one of the modes of communication:** one-way, two-way or fusion, and

⦾ **one of the types of boundaries:** rigid, flexible or blurred.

organizations. Throughout the book, the two circles are of equal size, but **on occasion, it would be correct to use differing sizes as a way of emphasizing the relative power of each**

of the parties, for example to indicate degree of authority, rank or responsibility, or political power. This graphic symbol helps clarify the message: if for example we wish to indicate that HQ's power is greater than that of employees in the field, we could enlarge the circle representing the HQ relative to that representing field staff, without any connection to the communication patterns between them.

In actuality, a specific system of interactions may involve more than two parties. Nonetheless, for the most part it's worth linking them in pairs and only afterwards, should it be necessary, present a more complex chart of all relationships. When analyzing the interactions between the development, production and marketing departments of an organization, for example, we can relate to the interactions between the development and production departments, between the development and marketing departments, and between the production and marketing departments, and thereafter relate to all of them simultaneously.

Let's now expand on each form of interaction.

(◎) Quality forms of interaction

Quality interactions are the synergy interaction itself and two additional forms which encourage synergy: interdependence and interfacing. If we wish to advance the process of creating synergy, we need to reinforce manifestations of these forms in the organization.

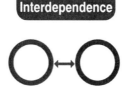

Interdependence links horizontally and is balanced. It reflects honest, quality and authentic dialogue between two equal parties where both benefit. Interdependence between two units in an organization is typified by a high frequency of interactions. This is a quality form, and of value to the organization since it promotes synergistic interactions. These will be described in more detail further on. Interdependence, however, requires a large degree of investment over the long term and is not always necessary or vital.

Interfaced

Interfaced is the second quality form, a state in which boundaries between the two parties are clear, although not necessarily highly flexible, and the two parties share fusing communication. A high level of interfaced interactions is characteristic of coordination meetings or board meetings, where members of the organization sit physically alongside each other and communicate with each other.

The interfaced form is not necessarily a state that creates synergy since it can also exist within rigid boundaries and does not require a reality of flexible boundaries, as synergy does (see below).

It's not always simple to differentiate between the forms of Interdependence and Interfaced, or between Interfaced and Synergy. The mathematical or graphic distinction is indicated by the fact that Interfaced indicates synergy at only one point. This is discussed in more detail at the end of the chapter.

Synergy is the form which allows the organization to create a new reality: it occurs as a result of the superimposition between the red and blue circles in the graph. The synergistic outcome can only result in an environment of flexible boundaries and fusing communication, and preserves the traits of the parts from which it came about, much like a child's unique DNA which nonetheless preserves the inherited data received from both parents.

Throughout this book, I've focused on the importance of synergistic interactions and creating synergy in the organization, but individuals may also enjoy its advantages if the form itself does not threaten the individual. If, on the other hand, the individual does feel threatened by it, the form will be experienced as invasive.

Any employee or staff member in an organization may experience the sense of satisfaction and calm that results from letting go of exhausting ego power plays, and the ensuing sense of release and relief from not having to "protect my boundaries." Letting go comes from the wish to improve the sense of trust and reduce conflicts among team members, together with a sense of personal gratification linked to shared working. The latter is often expressed as needing a sense of belonging, of receiving support, and being reinforced by other team members, assuming they too have made their ego boundaries more flexible. In such cases, there is also the sense of reward derived from chances for learning, and for an enjoyable, stimulating work environment.

The synergistic interaction is an ongoing process of re-creation. As an organization, we don't want to eradicate the units, departments, cultures or subsidiaries that gave rise to the new entity: rather, we want to reinforce them. We want the boundaries between them to be clear and not blurred, but we simultaneously want them to be sufficiently flexible to allow a constant renewal of synergy.

Let's return to the example of a couple wishing to begin a new family. On one hand, the boundary should be flexible, a boundary that allows constructive, open dialogue based on fusing communication. On the other hand, the two individuals must also have clearly defined roles. If, for example, one of them begins the workday later than the other, and is therefore able to prepare young children in the morning for kindergarten or school, then it is clear to both whose role that is, and there is no need to conduct negotiations on this issue every morning.

If the boundary between them is flexible, however, they can swap roles easily: for example, if the person who usually handles the kids' morning preparations is unable to on a particular day, or the one who doesn't normally do that simply wants to for a change, all it takes is a brief dialogue which won't cause any conflict: instead, it will strengthen the couple's relationship or, in our terminologies, reinforce their synergistic form.

Only from this stance can synergy exist between the two partners, allowing them to continue upholding and developing the family unit which they created, while simultaneously enabling each of the couple to grow and develop as individual entities. If neither a clear, flexible definition of boundaries nor any fusing communication exists between the partners, at least to a high degree, synergy will cease to exist and the family unit may well collapse.

Neutral forms of interaction

Neutral forms of interaction are neither positive nor negative but depend on the organizational structure or situation of the organization in which they operate. They particularly depend on the overall mix of interactions. Neutral forms tend to develop into destructive forms, however, so it's worth paying attention to their frequency of appearance within the mix of interactions. In other words, for as long as neutral interactions don't disrupt the organization's functioning and for as long as they don't create conflict or problems, they may remain neutral. This will be expanded on in Chapter 4 when we discuss reducing neutral interactions.

Hierarchy represents one-way communication, which is almost always a top down flow, or from the head office to the field, to various units or to employees in the organization. In this way, for example, procedures or guidelines are handed "down" from highest to lower ranks in the organization. Requiring employees to punch in their attendance cards on entering and exiting the workplace is a hierarchic interaction which is not based on dialogue or feedback: in other words, we do not expect the employee to agree, or disagree.

An organization may hold a dialogue with employees on improving or altering the procedure but for as long as the procedure remains in place, this type of communication pattern is one-way. Large complex organizations based on ongoing routine work benefit greatly from working with procedures, and generally do not encourage dialogue or communication of any kind with employees concerning these procedures.

Case Study

During my military service, I worked on instituting a change to weapons development procedure. The one-way procedure was on the verge of becoming part of the Chief of Staff's orders, but out of my natural affinity and fondness for synergistic processes, I found it important, at least at the level of creating the process, to create quality communication with the various military units about to adopt the procedure.

As a result, a very interesting thing happened: units in the field adopted the procedure even before the Chief of Staff signed it into effect. The procedure improved work effectiveness so much that at the level of the field, the statement was "We want it" even before the Chief of Staff had said, "This procedure obliges you to..."

We often assume that a one-way direction is the manifestation of a need from head office or the organization's administration, but in this case it was the people in the field who implemented and internalized the procedure, and preferred to use the shared language which the procedure created rather than continue operating in a reality of highly blurred boundaries.

No interaction is a form where no connection exists between two units or people in the organization. In large complex organizations, there may be work processes which do not require connections among all units or among employees, and no interaction would be considered a neutral form and non-impacting. But in cases where interaction is necessary yet does not exist, at least as a felt sense by one of the parties involved, then the situation can definitely be considered one of disconnectedness, a problematic state that may damage interactions and the possibility of creating organized synergy.

In multinational organizations operating online teams, for example, some employees may be operating from different time zones and the non-interaction between them is natural, simply because they work at different hours. A time-based disconnect of this kind would probably not be perceived as problematic. But if one of the team members went on vacation without informing others on the team, and wasn't answering email over a lengthy period, it could develop into a sense of disconnectedness among the other team members and even invasion.

This example demonstrates two points which I'll relate to further on: the first is that, at any given point in time, all forms of interaction coexist. Most of the time, team members maintain quality interactions, but occasionally need to cope with disconnection. The second point is that every form is judged subjectively: in other words, a team member's silence may be sensed as a disconnect more strongly by some and less so, or not at all, by others.

Among some team members a sense of invasion may develop if they feel that a procedure or norm of action has been breached, and the result is the sensation of threat. Some may react with "John always answers... there must be a reason for the delay" whereas others may react with "Who does John think he is? Why isn't he answering? Now his workload's falling on me and I can't get ahead with my own tasks!" The diversity of reactions derives from personal and personality traits as well as from the nature of the relationship between the 'silent' member and other team members.

Destructive forms of interaction

Destructive forms of interaction are those which do not enable the organization to create synergy, and in general prevent the organization from functioning well. These interactions can be diagnosed as organizational illnesses, and of course we need to avoid and reduce their appearance as far as possible. As will be seen further in this chapter, the questionnaire on forms of interaction relates to the strength of each form in percentages. Organizational illness is defined from a perception of 7% and up.

The two types of destructive forms, obscurity and invasion, are linked to boundaries and therefore any action which seeks to reduce them must occur through improved definitions of the organization's boundaries. More on this in Chapter 4.

Obscurity develops when the defined boundary between two units or functionaries in the organization is not sufficiently clear, or is lacking: for example, when there is no up-to-date definition of roles in the organization, or when there is no agreement between two functionaries concerning the definition of a role, for whatever the reasons may be.

As a result, procedures and instructions aren't carried out in actuality, which causes tangible damage to an organization's effectiveness. Additionally, a state of blurred boundaries harms the quality of interactions between employees and certainly does nothing towards creating synergy. See more on this in the previous chapter's discussion of blurred boundaries.

Invasion

Invasion occurs when an employee or functionary in the organization penetrates the sphere or function of another employee, despite the existence of clear boundaries between them. Invasion can occur at the personal, intra-unit or departmental level, or at the organizational level, such as with competition between organizations. In any case, the sense of invasion is subjective.

Frequently enough I find indications of invasive interactions specifically in sales departments. Sales staff tend to invade areas of functioning that do not belong to their territories, often due to the remuneration structure chosen by the organization, which includes personal bonuses and may additionally encourage competition and even cannibalism. When invasion occurs, it causes friction and conflict among employees, which prevents developing cooperation and synergy.

Two Case Studies

One of the first organizations where I worked as an organizational consultant was an industrial concern comprising six manufacturing plants. Each plant was one link in the production chain, with each one's produce being the raw materials for the next one. Some of the plants also sold to external clients. The organization's VP was a young and highly energetic manager, very loyal to the organization's objectives, so that when a plant manager didn't uphold the organization's targets, our young manager invaded that domain and took up what he saw as slack in the reins.

During that same period I developed and consolidated the synergy method, and when I began applying it to my work with the young manager, I explained the significance of the destructive form of invasion. To his credit, he didn't express any insistent opposition to my points, although he did offer some "reasons" for why he had "no choice" but to invade.

These kinds of rationales are typical of an individual invading a territory beyond her or his scope, but they don't necessarily derive from ego or needing control. Sometimes they come from an honest wish to assist: "he doesn't understand exactly what needs to be done," "they constantly mess up on that," or "she has to keep the clients happy, we can't afford to lose clients" are common phrases. That same VP, like many other managers, did not realize that by taking on responsibility for a role that belongs to someone else, he may not necessarily be helping that other person: on the contrary, usually it's just a disruption.

Only after working together on organizational interactions, and once I showed the young manager the graph in blue and red on white, did the penny drop. "I get what you're talking about now," he said, and together, we set out on developing a new path towards comprehensive synergy, which lessened invasion and enabled the manager to reinforce the plant manager by applying tools that allowed the latter to execute his job better.

*

In this second case, I participated in the process of developing managers in a bank, a process intended to train employees marked as potential candidates for managerial positions. When I presented the invasive interaction and its negative aspects, participants claimed that the bank's organizational and managerial culture viewed such behaviors in a positive light and even encouraged them: as one young participant explained, "If one employee invades the role of another, the bank's management looks at it as an indicator of having a "big thinker mindset," and a sure sign that the invading employee is capable of doing more than what the role's definition calls for, so it's seen as a good thing."

Of course, having flown the synergy banner on high, it wasn't easy for me to listen to these kinds of remarks. I made a mental note of this organizational "defect," which would be important to raise at the bank's board meeting, and asked the participants, "In your opinion, what percentage of invasion is there in the organization?" I was happy to hear estimates of between three to five percent, a reasonable figure which doesn't threaten the creation of synergy in the organization, even though it was definitely a figure worth reducing, especially among employees or units where it was more manifest.

In many cases I encounter sensations of invasion even when, in actuality, no manager or employee has invaded the role of any other. Since the feeling is subjective, there's no point in "explaining" to an employee that this sensation is mistaken, or in trying to understand its source. Usually it derives from the simple fact that each of us feels a need to protect our boundaries at some level, and this need may derive from gender, cultural or social differences, from an individual's emotional makeup, personality or the accrued experiences of life and the way that individual interprets them.

Case Study

In a large corporation I advised, the ERP program for organizational resource management was being assimilated. Employees received joint training sessions on using the software, followed by several hours allocated to personal training. One employee expressed dissatisfaction with the personal training and sharply criticized the trainer's behavior, to the point of conflict between them, and refusal to work together.

The phrasing that the employee used demonstrated the deep feeling of invasion she felt. Following a conversation with her, it became apparent that the trainer reminded her of her ex-husband both physically and in his mode of speech. The employee found it difficult to disengage from the sense of invasion she had felt as her marriage collapsed and during the process of divorce. But her ability to identify the reasons for her feelings helped us reduce her sense of invasion, because the personal element in communication between her and the trainer was neutralized. This also made it far easier for the trainer to understand that his difficulty in connecting with the employee was not any fault of his.

Two final notes about invasion:

Invasion is not necessarily active: people perceive invasion when they feel someone acts "out of the line", being impudent, brakes the rules, does not act according to the teams' culture etc.

The second point is that in many cases invasion is answered by invasion from the other party. Example for these two points: : Sara and Dave work together in a large architecture firm. One day Dave was late, which put Sara into a situation where she could not finish her task on time. When David finally arrived, Sara who is usually a very nice person, started screaming at him. David answered back, and the head of the office had to intervene to calm them down and have the work down. Analyzing the situation with all 3 of them showed invasion: all three of them perceived a high percentage of invasion. Sara felt David disrespect her anf her time. David felt that it was not for her to scold him, and the head of the office felt that her time had been invaded.

How do boundaries and communication patterns shape the 7 Forms of Interaction?

Now that the types of boundaries and communication patterns in the synergistic approach have been explained, and the 7 Forms of Interaction characterized, we can delve deeper into understanding how boundaries and communication patterns create the forms of interaction.

The chart below demonstrates and summarizes this issue. According to the synergy perception, three types of boundaries can be found in organizations: rigid, flexible and blurred; and three types of communication exist: one-way, two-way, and fusion.

Integrating them leads to 6 possible forms of interaction.

◐ According to the chart, when the boundary is blurred (more than 7% of experiences are perceived as blurred) it makes no difference what pattern of communication is used, the outcome will remain a feeling of obscurity. If the organization wishes to reach quality forms of interaction, it must first handle the blurred boundaries.

How Communication Patterns and Boundaries Shape the 7 Forms of Interaction

Communication Pattern → / Boundary ↓	One-Way	Two-Way	Fusion
Rigid	Hierarchy / Invasion	Interdependence	Interfacing
Flexible	Obscurity	Interfacing	Synergy / Overlap
Blurred	Obscurity	Obscurity	Obscurity

Chart 2: Creating forms of interaction from the types of boundaries and communication

◑ When boundaries are rigid and communication is one-way, hierarchy or invasion results. When boundaries are rigid and communication is two-way, interdependent interactions occur. When boundaries are rigid but fusing communication is used, an interfaced outcome is created.

◑ When the boundary is flexible but communication is one-way, obscurity eventuates; when boundaries are flexible and communication is two-way, interfaced occurs.

◑ Synergy is formed only when boundaries are flexible and the communication pattern is fusion.

◑ You've probably noticed that the form of no interaction does not appear in the chart. That's because it is not a form of interaction but rather, testifies to a lack of interaction. In a state of no-interaction there is no relationship at all between the two parties. However, one-way communication may also give rise to the sensation of no interaction when one party actually is attempting to interact but receives no response. If this situation is not improved, it is then likely to be perceived as invasion.

Differentiating the three types of quality forms

The quality forms of interaction are important enough to warrant delineating how they differ from each other.

First, note that the quality interactions form a square in the chart's upper right. In other words, when boundaries are blurred or communication is one-way, there are no quality interactions.

Synergy comes about only once in the nine possible convergences, whereas the other interactions may come about from several converging traits. This point is worthy of emphasis in light of the fact that synergy results from the convergence of a boundary pattern and a communication pattern which are tough to achieve: on one hand, it's hard to create flexible boundaries because those require a high level of self-confidence, alongside confidence in the other; and on the other hand, fused communication requires practice and trust from both parties.

Interdependence is the most commonly found form in organizations, to the point of being perceived as the dominant interaction. It can occur within rigid boundaries because it doesn't require flexing boundaries, and involves two-way communication. Interdependence is easier to achieve and preserve but does not allow creating a new reality. It's therefore considered good enough for most ongoing work needs within the organization.

Interfaced is a quality form that allows creating synergy but only at one point: at the point of interface. The question of whether something new is or isn't created from an interfacing interaction is subjective and open to interpretation by members of the work team and management. For example, if the work team's goal is to improve customer service, we could say that an improved outcome for customer service indicates the new synergistic reality which the organization sought to create by defining the task of the team focusing on how the organization's various units contribute to this effort.

Aspects of synergy

"A chain is no stronger than its weakest link."

So said the philosopher William James. His statement accurately reflects the essence of synergy because the synergistic approach contains multiple aspects, or links, which impact its formation, or the chain's strength. We can't create synergy if we don't relate to all these aspects, and if even one aspect is neglected, the chain of synergy could unravel.

Often, I've encountered a situation where clients viewed my work in organizational consultancy as a nice side dish to their organization, a bit like a training session or pep talk. However, the synergy method is far more than that. It's a total concept derived from applying its approach to businesses in the real world. Relating to the multiplicity of an organization's areas is important when seeking to create and apply a synergistic approach.

The synergistic concept impacts all areas of an organization, far beyond the field of human resources where an organizational consultant's work generally focuses. Synergy helps form better links between the various components that make up the organizational system, improves efficiency, and directly contributes to increasing a company's profits.

Let's take a look at the 7 main aspects of the synergy concept.

1. The strategic aspect
The strategic aspect addresses the issue of how far the organization's strategy is committed to creating a

new reality. During the course of my work, I came across many instances of mergers undertaken for the purpose of creating synergy between two companies. However, because of strategies which concealed information from the market, and as a result, also from employees, in actuality the companies ended up not realizing their purpose. I call this phenomenon the paradox of synergy. You'll have read it in detail in the introduction.

The case described below accurately reflects why it is important for organizational strategy to relate to diversity among the organization's units and learn of the need for creating synergy.

Case Study

A company in the field of logistics was conducting a process of splitting into several divisions, with substantial autonomy given to each division, as part of a new strategic program. When I began working with the company, it became apparent that the organization's split into divisions also split the units that had been subordinate to the human resources VP. Each unit had been transferred to a different division, so that the training manager was now part of one division, the remuneration unit was in another division, and so on.

The strategic plan had ignored the organization's need for synergistic solutions to address human resources management. The correct solution in this case would have been to leave the human resources unit in the organization's HQ. This would have ensured that all its activities were under one roof, from where it could provide services to the other divisions. An alternative would have been to create a synergistic communication pattern, such as a steering committee backed up by professional facilitation from a specialist from each of the other divisions. This solution would have promoted synergy among the units, even though at the formal level each human resources unit was subordinate to a different division. Addressing the situation this way is known as a matrix structure.

2. The structural aspect

Synergy's structural aspect primarily deals with

boundaries which relate to the quality of the organization's structure and job descriptions. This is where we must assure clarity when defining organizational subordination, tasks, responsibilities and powers, partners in the role, career patterns, and so on. On the other hand, we must allow for flexibility, which itself enables keeping ahead of the fast paced changes typical of our current business environment.

3. The procedural aspect

Synergy's procedural aspect deals with work processes, such as planning and production in the manufacturing plant, and the areas of decision making, coordination, remuneration and training in head offices. These are processes which usually cross the organizational structure and involve every department in an organization.

An organization's structural boundaries make it harder to transfer work processes among departments. It's important that these boundaries are crossed synergistically by ensuring that the boundaries themselves are clear and flexible. This will enable achieving cooperation from all departments in the organization, through fusing communication: in the decision making process, for example, brainstorming or masterminding tools are good choices. You can read more about brainstorming in the chapter on decision making in Organizational Behavior by Stephen Robbins and Timothy Judge.

4. The human aspect

The human aspect of synergy deals with the organization's human resources. The human aspect has far reaching influence on our ability to successfully create synergy. At the end of the day, we're dealing with relationships among people, no matter which aspect we're involved in, and behind every successful or failed outcome is the person or people who executed it.

I do want to emphasize that intra-organizational changes

can harm the employee's status, and cause a drop in the motivation or willingness to cooperate and adopt a change. The greater the fear and difficulty experienced by employees, managers and business partners, the more detrimentally affected their motivation will be, making it harder to achieve synergy in the organization.

Case Study

A good example of the impact that the human aspect has on creating synergy in the organization is the case of two business partners who inherited ownership of an industrial plant. One was the daughter of a founding partner, and the second was the son in law of another founding partner. For a lengthy period they managed the plant together but encountered no small number of problems. In fact, the daughter fell ill and ceased coming to the plant.

My role was to assist them in overcoming the personal difficulty in working together, and reduce the sense of invasion one of them felt. It was clear to me that for as long as the human aspect wasn't dealt with, there could be no forward movement in working on achieving synergy in any of the other areas. The partners absolutely had to find a way to work together synergistically in order to advance the entire organization. In this case, and in many others, the simple graphic forms enable the partners to realize the percentage of obscurity in the division of roles, and responsibilities between them. After clarification, both were able to concentrate on the diverse role each of them wanted to take in the plant. Once again they were able to see the potential for synergy between them.

5. The technological aspect

Synergy's technological aspect is linked to that of processes, and deals with assimilation of new technology. The synergy approach seeks to create dialogue and ongoing communication among all departments in the organization, and if software exists to help that along, it should be installed and assimilated in a way that assures optimal linkage across the organization.

Here are two situations which demonstrate the technological aspect in achieving synergy.

Two Case Studies

An academic institution began using ERP software for overall management of human resources in the organization. However, a year later, the organization's service providers were still incapable of responding to clients. They claimed that they still didn't fully understand how to use the program, and that it was causing them confusion and work delays. This example demonstrates how the introduction of a quality software program fails because of unsuccessful assimilation processes.

*

In this second case, ERP was assimilated into a very large multinational corporation. My role was to evaluate whether the program had been successfully assimilated. To my surprise I discovered that because the process had been conducted over several years, different divisions within the same organization were working with different programs .

It is important to note that this software essentially seeks to create dialogue among management programs in the organization's various divisions. Obviously, installation of different programs that can no longer "talk" to each other damages the program's very nature and purpose. Solving this major glitch meant conducting a complex, expensive and careful set of procedures geared at ensuring that all programs could talk with each other. Correct synergistic planning in advance would have prevented this time and energy wasting activity.

6. The legal aspect

This aspect deals with legal areas typical of an organization's work, such as contracts, employment agreements, complex customer complaints and so on. If we want to work synergistically in all areas of the organization, even work conducted with legal advisors must operate under synergistic principles.

A legal contract or agreement is a document intended to protect both parties, and therefore by its very nature, it creates rigid boundaries, whereas working synergistically seeks flexible boundaries, otherwise synergy cannot exist. A consultant's objective is to adapt all procedures and documents to the synergy approach. That includes formulation of contracts and agreements and ensuring that in those, too, flexible boundaries exist as far as possible, towards encouraging quality interactions.

7. The economic aspect

The synergistic economic aspect is linked to an organization's finances and has strong influence over the organization's profitability, as shown by the following case.

Case Study

In a large industrial organization which had undergone significant strategic and structural changes, including a transition to a profit center structure. Using a profit center structure meant that every production plant in the concern was now responsible for its own bottom line: in other words, its profitability.

When my diagnosis of the organization's interactions began, however, I discovered that despite the structural change, costing authority hadn't been decentralized. The main office's management had kept this aspect under its own control. Additionally, this organization worked with a small number of strategic clients, and costing of every order for every client was critical. In other words, each production plant had been defined as an independent and separate unit, but the plant's overall managerial level had not allowed any of them to cost their products without first receiving head management's okay. Worse yet, prices were also dictated to each plant by head management.

The main complaint coming in from plant managers was that the concern's management was interfering, or in synergy terms, invading, the area of product costing, making it impossible for them to accept responsibility for the plant's profitability. The solution I suggested was to work correctly from the economic aspect, which meant redefining plant managers' powers authority. This would inherently reduce the incidents of invasion and would simultaneously serve as a way of assimilating synergy in the organization.

Synergy in mergers and acquisitions (M&A): Starting out on the right foot

The following examples demonstrate the synergistic aspects relative to processes of M&A between two different organizations.

Strategic: in most mergers, at least at the outset of the process, the strategy is to conceal the fact that a merger is occurring, which leads organizations to taking synergy on board only in relatively late stages of the merger. My advice is always to take into account that hiding the merger contributes to rigidifying the boundaries and a feeling among employees of invasion. This is an example where there is an imminent contradiction between the strategic and the human aspects of strategy. According to the synergy approach, this is a major reason for the poor M&A success statistics.

Structural: mergers usually require changes to organizational structure. Typically, units may merge, may be eradicated, or new units may be established. As a result, definitions of purpose at the level of unit, and definitions of role at the level of the individual employee, may also alter. These changes should be reviewed synergistically, examining how they can integrate into a fabric of optimally functioning vital connections, while aiming to prevent the creation of sensations of blurring and invasion that structural changes can cause.

Processes: re-planning processes following a merger have important influence. For example, each organization has its unique sales process for its particular products or services. Integrating the processes synergistically should take into account the strengths of each sales process, the remuneration system for sales staff, and so on. This is also true for other organizational processes such as human resources, especially relative to remuneration, training, and manager development, which gain a central focus in synergistic mergers or acquisitions. In actuality, however, we find that the acquiring organization frequently forces its processes on the acquired organization. Doing this inherently disregards the acquired organization's sales processes and will most likely cause those employees to feel invaded by the acquiring party.

Human: the impact of the human factor on creating processes of synergy between two organizations boils down to a basic question: what is the personal significance of the merger for each of the organization's managers and employees?

Ignoring this human aspect may cause a feeling of invasion among employees, and evident efforts at maintaining their boundaries, inherently making the creation of synergy more difficult. Relating to the human aspect promotes creative thinking relative to the people involved, and gives space to human decency in the merger. This is even truer for a merger announcement which comes to employees, and sometimes even to senior management, as a complete surprise. Senior managers know that employees may need to be calmed, but they occasionally try to achieve this through the tool of coercion, which will usually backfire because it will be perceived by employees as invasive and lead to conflict that could have been avoided.

Technological: an example of the impact of technology on creating synergy in a merger between two organizations can be seen when decisions need to be taken on software programs which had been used by each of the organizations prior to their merger. These include ERP, CRM, accounting programs, and more. The question usually raised is: how to determine which program to continue? The decision is often based on considerations of cost, quality, and suitability of the program to the post-merger organization's needs.

When managing mergers according to the synergy approach, however, consideration must be given to the fact that some employees may oppose adapting to technological changes. In one such case, employees accustomed to working with a particular program were forced to switch to another. They found it hard to assimilate the new program, which in synergistic terms is described as a feeling of invasion, making it more difficult to achieve assimilation of the new program, let alone organizational synergy. You'd be surprised to discover the many methods employees, who feel their boundaries have been invaded, can devise for delaying, if not utterly avoiding, adaptation to the new software.

Legal: the impact on the merger process of the way that legal contracts are formulated. A synergistic approach would word merger contracts to preserve clear boundaries yet ensure that no overly rigid boundaries are created. Mechanisms for discussing differences of opinion can also be used as a way of ensuring that all viewpoints are expressed.

The merger or acquisition contract is just one of the initial two-way steps for linking companies. From my experience, a merger does usually create boundaries which are too rigid, making it harder to achieve synergy. My advice is to emphasize to the lawyers drawing up the contracts that the strengths of each organization should be focal to the contract's formulation. In cases where a consultant, human resources expert or organizational development specialist from within the organization is brought on board, it is worth integrating that person into the legal contract formulation process.

Economic: considerations of profitability, the reason behind a merger, influence the merger process. Economic issues manifest in decisions linked with profitability: how production and operational processes can be streamlined to advance synergy without losing important knowledge held by each of the companies. Achieving this means avoiding situations where:

- Decisions are taken based on political power or ego;
- It is unclear who holds authority to take certain decisions;
- Decisions are not taken in close proximity to "the client": in other words, they are made at ranks too senior for the type of decision, or made by the acquiring company relative to clients of the acquired company.

If these kinds of situations aren't avoided, synergy cannot be successfully achieved, and profitability will not be maximized. In extreme cases, the merger will fail.

Summary: an organization operating synergistically is a strong, effective and efficient one, where work on creating synergy occurs in all its fields and for all aspects based on the understanding that the strengths of each link in the organizational chain must be preserved, and based on the knowledge that neglecting even one aspect may break the chain.

⦿ Important pointers for creating synergy

Now that we understand the patterns which exist within the 7 Forms of Interaction Model, their importance for creating synergy, and what aspects need to be related to in the assimilation process, we can review the four important pointers we need to be aware of before beginning to embed synergy in the organization as a whole.

1. In any given situation all forms concurrently exist

The first pointer I wish to review is the fact that in

any given situation, all forms of interaction concurrently exist in the organization. It is worth keeping in mind that organizations are dynamic bodies exposed to diverse influences and subject to changes, which is why no single form can exist 100% of the time.

In fact, all seven forms exist in organizations. What differentiates a successful organization from one finding it hard to reach its targets, is the mix of forms. In other words, in reality we encounter manifestations of synergy despite the existence of neutral or destructive forms.

In the introduction, you read that implementing the synergy method is possible in two dimensions: a containing or enabling dimension, or a coercive and constraining dimension. A merger, for example, can come about following a hostile takeover. It is fairly reasonable to assume that feelings of invasion and obscurity will manifest among employees and managers of the organization that has been taken over. This can also be expected in some of the acquiring organization's employees, who may find themselves suddenly demoted in favor of incoming employees. In such cases it is doubtful that synergy could be created between the two organizations, but we can still achieve a level of synergy in some percentage, despite the coercive move.

When discussing issues with managers or employees working to create synergy in an organization, they tend to disproportionately stress what bothers or disrupts them the most at that moment in time; alternately, they stress synergistic interactions and ignore others. In social studies this phenomenon is called the halo effect. It focuses on one dominant aspect and avoids relating to other communication norms.

In the introduction I mentioned my work in the Hadassah Women's Organization in Israel, and the process of synergy I was asked to create between two diverse groups of volunteers. At the time, I called synergy "the purple form" because of the color created between the red and blue interfacing circles. At some point while working on developing synergy between them, a board member said, "Look, Hadassah's becoming a purple organization."

I was very apprehensive about the negative impact of this encompassing statement on the synergistic process. It was important for me to stress that we don't want the organization to "go purple" but to create a new reality while simultaneously maintaining the nature of the two powerful cultures within the organization, that of the American-based parent organization and that of the local volunteers.

This example also demonstrates how reinforcing synergy, primarily in complex organizations, can have a local flavor without impacting the entire organization. In this way, synergy can be improved in a specific task force without the organization's culture being altered. As I will show in the third pointer, synergy comes at a high price, and it isn't easy to be in a constant state of synergy, nor is there any need. We should empower the synergistic mode only when we want to create a new reality; and even then, other forms will continue to exist, as will be shown in pointer 4 below.

2. The level of a perceived interaction is subjective

The second pointer relates to the subjectivity with which every manager or employee in an organization perceives an interaction and its power. Different people will perceive the same mix of interactions differently. Subjectivity derives from each individual's character, feeling, knowledge and personal experience. When we work on synergy in an organization, there is no need to try and instill one single "objective" truth. In fact, we are prohibited from attempting to do this. Instead, it is very important to respect and understand each employee's subjective perception of any interaction.

An example would be if one manager claimed that another manager at a senior, parallel or subordinate position was invading her or his role. It makes no difference if the "accused" manager feels like an invader or not; work needs to be done with that manager on understanding how she or he is perceived as invasive, and what that implies. The "invader" doesn't need to agree or accept the claim, but just acknowledge that it derives from diversity, and understand its consequences. Incidentally, a state of invasion is usually characterized as one felt by the invaded party and not the invading party, which emphasizes just how clearly the sensation is subjective. Organizations with a strong political culture might view invasion as a legitimate way to achieve personal or departmental goals.

Throughout my years of work with the Synergy Method, I was involved in dozens of organizational projects, but only once came across a manager who was able to identify himself as an invader. In fact he was a commander of a police station who, after receiving the results of the diagnostic questionnaire, understood on his own to what degree he had overshot his role and invaded areas of responsibility delegated to his subordinates, by taking on some of their roles.

Most managers tend to tag their organization as being far more synergistic than their lower level employees do. Every time I start working with a new organization, I work top to bottom "top down". First I work with the organization's management, distributing questionnaires to them which request them to mark the interactional mix in the organization, and only afterwards I begin reviewing departments and teams.

My experience shows that most managers ascribe high percentages to the quality interactions: synergy, interfaced and two-way. But when I pass the questionnaire out to subordinates, very different data come back, usually a good deal less positive.

What does this indicate about managers? Are they disconnected from reality? Not necessarily. They believe in all honesty that they're creating synergy in their organizations. We all know that phrase, "The neighbor's grass is always greener." It turns out that employees experience far more obscurity and lack of clarity, invasion and one-way interactions than their managers do.

But it's also very important to keep in mind that creating synergy in the organization is not a witch hunt looking for whom to blame. Organizations that hire the services of an organizational consultant for the sake of trying to pinpoint who is right and therefore, by corollary, who is blameworthy, or that expect the organizational consultant to achieve "organizational justice," will never succeed in creating a meaningful level of synergy.

Together with the realization that the mix of forms is subjective, it is worth noting that it's possible to incorporate improvement vis-à-vis the overall perception of a form, irrespective of how that form is perceived by any specific manager or employee. Let's take, for example, a unit of 10 employees. The majority indicate that in 7% of situations, they feel their manager is invasive. The invasive interaction in this case will be handled very differently to a situation where 9 of the employees rate invasion with a very low percentage and just one employee gives it a high rank. For more details on this aspect see chapter 4 on how the appearance of destructive forms in the organization can be reduced.

3. The price of synergy

Synergy is vital to creating a new reality in the organization but, as with every change, it has its price. Understanding the meaning of this price requires keeping in mind that reinforcing synergistic interactions needs cooperation of a kind that managers and employees are not accustomed to, and may therefore be perceived as a threat. It's also a process that crosses organizational structures and cultures, which further raises its price and at least initially, increases difficulties. But the return on investment (ROI) for reinforcing synergy should be far more than its cost, and this is indeed the result when synergy is correctly assimilated.

Time is the first, and most significant, cost of creating synergy. Making boundaries more flexible and improving communication among members of an organization requires a large amount of managers' time. How often I hear claims such as, "There are so many meetings that there's no time to work..." and it's true: improved interactions in general, and creating synergy in particular, require the organization's leadership to devote a great deal of attention to the process, and be wholly committed.

Next comes the discomfort felt during the embedding of change. Most managers and employees are not used to thinking synergistically. Additionally, easing boundaries is perceived as threatening, especially to the ego, since boundaries are meant to protect and ensure a feeling of safety. Discomfort as a sensation differs from one person to another, and depends on personality. The level of perceived discomfort is wholly subjective.

Lastly, the process of change requires coping with issues linked to ego, power, organizational politics and loyalty in interactions, embodied by questions such as: am I loyal to my role, or to the new synergistic outputs? How do I split my time between defined tasks pertaining to my role, and actions that benefit my unit or the entire organization?

4.   When is it correct to use synergy?

We use synergy to create a new reality.

Look how simply the rule can be stated. But implementation is far from simple. Just what is that new reality, when organizations in current times experience such frequent changes?

This is the perfect opportunity to distinguish between first level change, which is quantitative only, and second level change, which relates to the essence of the organization and results from the formation of something new and different.

Some months ago I was invited to consult for a legal office specializing in relocation: handling Israelis who wish to work abroad or international experts coming to work in Israel. As in many legal offices, this one was also based on several areas of specialization, each department headed by a lawyer whose expertise was in a specific field. The managing partner presented the problems he was coping with as office manager, including his difficulty in getting cooperation from several departments in a new niche which still had no "guiding hand," that is, a defined department head.

The need for cooperation to promote the new area is an example of a situation where a synergistic interaction can shape a new reality. Note that the office manager didn't present me with quantitative problems such as difficulty in simultaneously handling a growing number of clients, or overload on incoming calls. Problems of that nature don't necessarily require reinforcement of synergistic interactions.

Sometimes a growth in the amount of work is so intrinsic that significant changes to the organization are necessary, such as redefining work process or roles, establishing or changing an organizational HQ, and so on. Because it's not always right to pay the price of strengthening synergy, the key question becomes: can the change be carried out in the current structure, or is a fundamental cultural, structural or procedural change needed first, and only afterwards should we review how to introduce the synergistic approach in general, and which forms to reinforce in particular.

At this point, it's valuable to discern between synergy as a managerial concept, and synergy as a form of interaction. Synergy as a managerial approach is beneficial to every organization wanting to encourage productive cooperation and willing to pay the price, primarily in terms of time, for the sake of increasing "soft" indexes such as gratification, motivation, innovation and creativity at the organizational and personal levels, or in order to see increases in "hard" indexes such as improved work processes, effectiveness, and profitability.

Strengthening synergy would be correct in the following situations:

◑ **Strengthening synergy interactions in the organization's administration.** The management of a division, profit center, or any relatively independent unit in the organization would be considered the organization's administration. It must operate as a synergistic team, because it embodies and represents the organization's functional diversity. An organization whose admin is not operating synergistically is doomed to fail.

◑ When the organization is facing far reaching changes, and / or when the organization has set strengthening interactions and team work as one of its primary objectives.

◑ Inserting changes that cross numerous organizational functions or are not in the field of authority of any organizational function. An example would be in mergers or acquisitions, cultural changes such as improvements to customer service or embedding a new managerial approach, technological or strategic changes such as penetrating new markets or altering the mix of products, and so on.

◑ **Units important to creating synergistic solutions and creativity**, such as R&D departments, quality improvement teams, projects teams or special tasks, brainstorming teams.

◑ In organizations specializing in knowhow or knowledge creation.

Applying the synergy method would be less appropriate in organizations operating in structured production or service processes executed without any essential connection among employees other than in cases or places where innovation is required, or in times of crisis.

Questionnaire for Self-Completion: 7F Model – 7 Forms of Interaction

Having dug deep into the synergy method, the time has come to test out completing the questionnaire. I want you to gain optimal benefits from it, so please read the following explanation first.

◖ This questionnaire aims to self-diagnose interactive forms in your organization. It is presented at this stage so that you can practice using it to implement improvements in your organization.

◖ The questionnaire assesses interactions in the work environment and not at the level of interpersonal relationships in other areas of content. See Chapter 3 on using the questionnaire: "The work process: Diagnostic stage."

◖ Note: the questionnaire carries copyright. You may use it for personal needs or to analyze the interactions among your employees on condition that you have read this book and internalized its content. Use of this kind does not infringe on copyright.

◖ The questionnaire is no more than a minimal level sample of the type of questionnaires I use, but optimal results are best assured, especially among large work forces, when the questionnaire is adapted to the organization's reality.

◖ The 7 Forms of Interaction Model Questionnaire is updated periodically. You can find the updated version in user friendly downloadable A4 format on www.ben-yshai.com

More tips for using the 7 Forms of Interaction Model Questionnaire

◑ It is important to encourage people filling in the questionnaire to provide examples for each type of petition related to in the questionnaire. Statements such as "everything works synergistically among us" are not acceptable, and in actuality usually conceal deeper issues which need to be accessed.

◑ As the questionnaire guidelines note, only after examples have been given for each form do we ask respondents to relate in terms of percentages. It is incorrect and counterproductive to mark percentages down first: from my experience, that is far too complex since the perception of any form is subjective. *It is easier for respondents to perceive a form in terms of a percentage when they can reread and compare all their described examples.*

Keep in mind that percentages reflect a subjective feeling; therefore, it is not important for them to be precise in order for you to get a pretty good idea of their distribution. It is important that the percentages allocated total 100%, and if they don't, encourage the participant to make adjustments by increasing or decreasing percentages to reach 100%. A total of 100% is necessary to allow a comparison of questionnaires, but there's no need to insist if deviation is up to 3% in either direction (totals of 97% to 103%).

7 FORMS OF INTERACTION MODEL – QUESTIONNAIRE

1. Think about the most important task, you have to carry out on your job, in the near future. *What is the task?*

_____

_____

_____

_____

2. Think about someone, with whom you have to collaborate to fulfill this task. *How are you related to this person: is she / he a business partner, co-worker, boss, client, etc?*

_____

_____

_____

_____

3. How good is your relationship with that person (please circle)?

Very Bad	Bad	Average	Good	Very good	Excellent

4. Give examples to every form of Interaction with that person. One circle represent you and one - the other person. Relate to your perceptions of the Interaction, not what "should have been". Do not feel in the percentages at this stage.

Interdependence	Interdependence – Dialog

Intensity of the form in %

Interfaced	Interfaced - Very good interaction (teamwork)

Intensity of the form in %

Synergy	Synergy - Very good interaction – supports creating something new
Intensity of the form in %	
Hierarchy	Hierarchy – Instructions are given; no feedback is expected
Intensity of the form in %	
No Interaction	No Interaction even though some is needed
Intensity of the form in %	

Obscurity	Obscurity – Parts of the boundaries (e.g. job description) are missing. Responsibilities are not well defined.

Intensity of the form in %

Invasion	Invasion – Though boundaries are well defined, one of you is invading the role of the other.

Intensity of the form in %

5. The percentages demonstrate the intensity of the form. For example, if you feel that Obscurity occurs often and disturbs you a lot, while Invasion is fairly rare, you may give 30% to Obscurity and only 5% to Invasion. Please ensure the total percentages for all 7 Forms together is 100%.

6. Your remarks

The 7 Forms of Interaction Model Questionnaire for Self Completion

Summary and your personal workbook

In this chapter you've studied the 7 Forms of Interaction in organizations. In the next chapter we will look at how to succeed in embedding synergy, and relate to its principles and the process. At this stage, I recommend mapping the mix of interactions in your organization by using the questionnaire and recording your impressions and remarks for each of the forms.

QUALITY FORMS
Interdependence

_____

_____

_____

_____

Interfaced

_____

_____

_____

_____

Synergy

_____

_____

_____

_____

NEUTRAL FORMS
Hierarchy

_____

_____

_____

_____

No Interaction

_____

_____

_____

_____

DESTRUCTIVE FORMS
Obscurity

_____

_____

_____

_____

Invasion

_____

_____

_____

_____

ASPECTS OF THE SYNERGY METHOD
The Strategic Aspect

_____

_____

_____

The Structural Aspect

_____

_____

_____

The Procedural Aspect

_____

_____

_____

The Human Aspect

_____

_____

_____

The Technological Aspect

_____

_____

_____

The Legal Aspect

_____

_____

The Economic Aspect

_____

_____

_____

IMPORTANT EMPHASES FOR CREATING SYNERGY
In any given situation, concurrently all forms exist

_____

_____

_____

_____

The level of a perceived interaction is subjective

_____

_____

_____

_____

The price of synergy

_____

_____

_____

_____

When is it correct to use synergy

_____

_____

_____

_____

THE 7 FORMS OF INTERACTION MODEL QUESTIONNAIRE
for SELF COMPLETION
Do you have general remarks? Do you have remarks
regarding the questionnaire?

_____

_____

_____

CHAPTER 3
How to successfully embed the synergy process

In this chapter we'll look at critical areas where the synergy process can be successfully assimilated.

The first half will present the components for successful assimilation. These components bring the previous chapter's content into closer focus, allowing you to progress to the work process further on. In order to adapt the components to your organizational reality, I suggest you turn to the table on page 100 and write down the degree to which each characteristic I present exists in your organization. In this way, you'll be able to get a better idea of which characteristics need changing and which should be preserved.

The second half of this chapter reviews the work process: that is, the stages which need to be implemented to improve interactions and create synergy. In addition, I will explain how to plan, execute and maintain the process, and how to balance between the need to create synergy, and the need to successfully cope with the daily reality in your organization. At the chapter's end you will also find work pages.

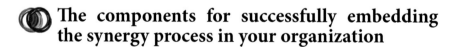 The components for successfully embedding the synergy process in your organization

1. Defining the purpose which links to the organization's vision

Successfully assimilating the synergy process in your organization requires you to define the purpose of the assimilation process, which is what you want to achieve, and to focus on a target that can be reached only through the synergy process, which is the new organizational reality we are trying to create.

As an example, if one of the organization's objectives, as an outcome of its vision, is to improve customer satisfaction, no department can achieve that on its own. This is a target which requires synergistic cooperation among all departments.

2. Creating commitment

Successfully creating synergy in the organization requires commitment to the process on the part of the organization's proprietors and managers, first of all, but also on the part of employees. The best status is for the organization to appoint someone with managerial authority as responsible for the role. This should preferably be a proprietor, chairperson or CEO who is totally committed and will motivate everyone else towards achieving that objective. If the person designated as responsible is not at the pyramidal apex, active support for the synergy assimilation process must be promised by the person in top position as well as involvement on the part of the organization's apex.

3. Defining and agreeing on boundaries

Creating synergy successfully in your organization requires you to define relevant boundaries among board members, partners, departments, employees, and so on; and to ensure, as far as possible, that everyone agrees to these boundaries. Any lack of agreement may lead to a blurring of boundaries, making it tougher to improve the quality forms, and putting the ability to create synergy at particular risk. As long as a high level of blurred boundaries exists, defined as more than 7%, or there is no agreement on boundaries, you need to work towards reducing blurring. See the next chapter for details on how to achieve this.

4. Acknowledging the importance of diversity and respecting the other

Synergy is based on diversity. Coping successfully with manifestations of diversity in the organization means respecting the other's difference, understanding it, learning what it derives from, what its scope is, and what characterizes it.

This is not an issue of agreement or disagreement. It is simply an acknowledgment of another's rationales. And this is where any activity which can help teach about the other, whether in the employment framework or out of it, comes into play. The purpose is to learn to live with diversity, understand its contribution to creating synergy, and promote the organization by relating to that diversity as a challenge rather than a threat.

Case Study

When working with the Hadassah organization, I wanted to improve familiarity between the group of English speaking volunteers and the group of Hebrew speaking volunteers. We held joint workshops for members of both groups based on regions, although in some areas such as main cities, two groups were run simultaneously, one for English speakers and another for Hebrew speakers.

As an Israeli, I was more readily identified with the Hebrew speakers' group. Wanting to ensure equality, I asked the international HQ's VP, who was in charge of developing membership in the USA, to facilitate the workshops together with me.

In the workshop's first half, we split participants into two groups based on cultural background. English speakers were facilitated by the VP, and Hebrew speakers by me. Each group was asked to define three points: how they would describe a successful year, what the group's strengths and weaknesses are, and what they consider as the other group's strengths and weaknesses.

In the workshop's second half, which I facilitated bilingually, each group presented its results. In this way we could bring the diversity to the surface, on one hand, while also observing how the different aspects could complement each other when creating successful projects based on the strengths of both groups.

I wrote a skit to close the workshop. It was performed by two volunteers, one from each culture, and demonstrated the stages in creating synergistic cooperation.

5. Synergy is not necessarily about chemistry

Creating synergy does not require the existence of interpersonal chemistry among the partners to the interaction. But good chemistry can make creating synergy easier. We can, however, reach synergy with people we don't feel any click with, and even with people we see as adversaries, as long as an understanding exists between us that the need to create synergy in the organization is of greater importance than any difference or absence of chemistry among us.

The more the organization's employees practice operating according to the Synergy Method, the more they'll be open to productive cooperation, both with people who are dissimilar, and with people whose views actively conflict with their own. You probably remember my statement in the introduction that synergy can be achieved through one of two dimensions: enabling and inclusion, which are based on interpersonal chemistry; or coercion and enforcement.

Our goal is to reach a state where every employee will be aware of the advantages of the new reality and how it will impact her or him. This makes employees more willing to rise above their habitual behavior and strengthen the synergistic interaction. For example, we often find parliament members from opposing parties submitting laws jointly, despite the lack of political chemistry between them, and sometimes despite the absence of any interpersonal chemistry. Peace agreements are a good example of such activity, since a new reality is created despite the absence of any chemistry on both sides. If creating synergy is possible for the purpose of achieving peace accords, how much easier it should be to achieve synergy within an organization, or between organizations.

The Israeli political system comprises numerous small parties and coalitions are often required to form a government, despite differing ideologies. In my work with politicians, I was surprised at their ability to link through a shared vision, such as legislating social laws, despite being bitter political rivals. Furthermore, real links sometimes developed between politicians of rival parties. Some say this points to the cynicism in the world of politics. I see it as the ability to read the map correctly, and join forces as a way of driving legislation they believe in. In other words, a new reality (legislation) is created by integrating conflicting forces, on one hand, but which share a specific shared vision, on the other, and reading the potential in these forces correctly. This example shows how a synergy bubble is formed.

Reducing manifestations of inequality in hierarchy

Successfully assimilating the synergy process means advancing lateral relations with members of the organization and avoiding linear relations. In other words, we should create non-linear hierarchy, one which produces order but does not necessarily stress the linear ranks within the organization.

Reducing expressions of inequality relative to the position of an employee or manager in the organizational hierarchy is a necessary condition for creating synergy. In organizational or managerial structures and cultures which are strongly hierarchic, tension may rise between the functionaries at different levels, resulting in difficulty in communication and cooperation among them. **We need to devote resources to learning the synergy perception and creating an explanatory platform which allows all participants to freely express themselves as individuals, rather than as representatives of the role they fill or the rank they hold.**

Synergy can be created among team members of different ranks if meetings are not held exclusively in the offices of the most senior ranking employee, as usually occurs in most organizations. Meetings can definitely be held in alternative locations, such as where lower ranking employees are stationed, including requesting every 'host', or any other participant, to summarize the meeting or discussion.

Case Study

A project I was involved in required structuring a new military remunerations system. It was very important to me that a range of role holders of various ranks were included, covering all departments and divisions. Anyone with a military background knows how difficult it is for sergeants to express themselves freely in front of senior officers. I worked at creating an environment where the lack of equality among participants was less dominant, and asked the team members to attend meetings dressed in civilian clothing. Unfortunately I wasn't able to convince participants to forego their external markers of rank, which were an inseparable part of the organizational culture, and as a result, meetings preserved the atmosphere of otherness instead of moving towards synergy.

6. Being simultaneously different yet equal

This component is an extension of the previous one, and emphasizes how a reduction of hierarchic manifestations leads to equality but not necessarily to uniformity. Most people tend to make a direct link between diversity and hierarchy. In other words, if there is difference between us, my natural tendency would be to check whether I'm better than you, or you're better than me, via our positioning on the "scale of comparison." That approach is a recipe for certain failure of the synergy process.

Often, when I raise the issue of difference, such as between male and female managerial styles, the discussion gets rowdy and raises resistance, especially on the part of women who perceive the discussion itself as discriminatory and insulting. But it's important to understand that the wish to rectify and maintain a society or organization as egalitarian, without ranking men or women, is not linked to the issue of difference. Differences exist, and will continue to exist, even in an equal society, and they are also vital for creating synergy which, in its essence, is based on creating something new by merging and integrating two different elements.

This principle is especially important in large organizations that tend to have a hierarchic organizational structure with rigid boundaries. The basic framework for creating a non-hierarchic structure is the steering committee or task force which crosses the organizational structure's breadth and height, and which we'll discuss in more detail in the next chapter.

7. Facilitation, staff development and management skills

The synergy method is a new language, so it needs to be taught to managers and employees. This can be done as part of a process of change or routine, for developing management trainees, in other training frameworks, or as a tool in the manager's toolbox. An example of a workshop conducted as part of the assimilation process appears in Chapter 4 above, dealing with acknowledging the importance of difference, and respecting the different individual. Another example was discussed in Chapter 2, on page 59, in the discussion on the concept of invasion, where I presented a case study demonstrating the development of a future management pool in a bank. In that case, the synergy method was studied by potential future managerial staff while demonstrating interactions among managers in head office and branch managers.

8. Remuneration according to the synergy approach

In many organizations, the remunerations system encourages personal excellence, expressed as bonuses according to the employee's achievements. It is important to remember that if such a system exists in your organization, particularly if it remunerates on the basis of serial rank in achievement, it may make the process of assimilating synergy much more difficult, because synergistic work is based on team effort and not personal achievement. If you wish to continue incentivizing your employees, I suggest using tools of team or organization-wide bonuses.

Case Study

A fascinating project I participated in involved working jointly with community nurses in Scotland. The nurses voluntarily took upon themselves, as part of the process of change, a central role in creating a joint pool of community resources such as lists of physicians, specialist clinics, and patient referrals to the appropriate clinics, based on patient needs.

During the first year, satisfaction was very high and the nurses functioned excellently. The second year saw a significant drop in functioning. In retrospect, it became clear that a large part of this activity took place in the nurses' free time. Many nurses experienced this as invasion and energetically "defended their boundaries." In other words, the organization did not remunerate them for this work, causing them frustration, significant loss of motivation, and reduced output. A deeper examination interestingly revealed that the sense of invasion was aroused or, at the least, empowered, by nurses' partners, who experienced the nurses' absence on weekends as ongoing involvement with their regular area of employment.

This situation demonstrates how interactions impact the circles and functions of others, outside the involved party's immediate employment and career. As soon as we identified the source of the problem, we were able to redefine the remuneration system and slotted staff meetings into the nurses' formal work hours. This change instantly affected the nurses' satisfaction as well as their outputs.

Exercise: Identify components in your organization

Having reviewed the vital components needed for improving organizational synergy, I recommend that you use the table below to write down the degree of relevance of each component for your organization's reality: to what level it exists or is absent, and what you feel must be maintained, reinforced or altered.

Success component	To what degree is this component present in your organization, and what are you going to change?
1. Defining a goal and linking it to the organization's vision	
2. Creating commitment	
3. Defining and agreeing on boundaries	
4. Acknowledging the importance of diversity and respecting the different	
5. Synergy is not "chemistry"	
6. Reducing manifestations of power inequality	
7. Being different but of equal value	
8. Facilitation, team development and management skills	
9. Remuneration based on the synergy approach	

The work process in 6 Stages: How to plan, execute and preserve the process of improved interactions in the organization

Filling in the table at the end of this chapter, on page 115 will help adapt the process to your organizational reality.

If you intend to execute this process on your own, I strongly recommend reading the book to its end, working through the exercises, and answering all the questions. This book is a work tool created for your use, and you're invited to underline, highlight, or write down anything that can help you before you undertake the process itself.

Additionally, allow me to remind you of all the aspects of synergy presented in the previous chapter, along with my recommendation to integrate them at each and every stage, and of course to relate to them according to their importance for your organization.

Before we commence, you need to decide whether you want to create a new reality, or whether improving existing interactions among employees is sufficient. Creating a new reality can occur, for example, when a merger takes place between organizations, or between units in an organization; when developing or improving a specific area of organizational activity, such as customer service; or when the organization seeks to penetrate new markets or launch a new product, and so on.

In the work stages described below, I relate to the process of creating a more in-depth new reality, one that requires a higher level of implementation. Before delving into the description, however, I wish to note that it's possible to achieve effective results in a relatively shorter and more focused process dealing with one specific area. If you wanted to improve synergy between board members, for example, you could have them join a short process with a high level of effectiveness.

Another example would be increasing the synergy form in the area of customer service: let's say this is a specific area you've identified which requires increasing the speed of reaction to clients.

In this case, you would hold two meetings. In the first, you can present the synergy approach to management, pass the questionnaire out to participants, and ask them to offer examples of the various forms. With the meeting's close you would interview each board member based on the questionnaire she or he filled out, and then analyze the questionnaires and prepare feedback.

In the second meeting you would present board members with the feedback and together with them, based on conclusions reached from this feedback, build an "improvement-based work plan" which you would write down, including a definition of goals, division of roles, points for evaluation, and review of progress.

Note that this process stresses progress along two axes simultaneously:

◍ **What needs to be done?** This relates to the improved output that interests the organization, which in this instance is the need to speed up reactions to clients; and

◍ **How to do it?** This axis encompasses improving interactions among employees involved in that sphere.

Integrating the two axes characterizes the synergy approach.

Now we'll take a closer look at the process of change by examining all its stages in depth.

I always recommend working in a considered, balanced way with this process: on one hand, ensuring that each of the six stages described below is applied with precision; on the other hand, adapting the process to your organization's needs and the resources available to you.

In retrospect, there seems to be a contradiction here, but

this isn't necessarily so: since you're the one controlling the reins, you're the person most familiar with your organization's limitations and needs, and you therefore know whether the process suits your organization or whether the organization lacks sufficient resources to implement any of its stages. But aiming to bite off more than we can chew is always self-defeating. Sometimes, then, it's preferable to go for a shorter or less in-depth process than forego the entire process altogether.

Here are the six stages of the synergy process.

1. Initial diagnosis and planning

I recommend conducting an initial diagnosis which includes responding to basic issues on the minds of people in your organization, such as: Why are we taking these steps? What new reality do we want to reach? Who are the players impacting it? Who can be expected to support the process, who will be neutral, and who might we expect to resist the process? The following are the issues that need to be considered at this stage.

◍ What is the objective?

The first step in the planning stage is to agree, first on the new reality we want to achieve, which is synergy; second, on the objective or target we're aiming for; and third, as far as possible, how to achieve it.

Case Study

When working on a merger between two companies in the field of finance, a service survey was conducted shortly after the merger. We identified that for some clients of the post-merger organization, a sense of reduced closeness was felt compared to the pre-merger state. Obscurity, no interaction and one-way communication patterns were also found: particularly among clients not knowing who to approach, and when they did make contact, their calls were not returned and issues remained unaddressed.

We focused on improving customer service, while emphasizing the preservation of a personal touch despite the merger. The new organization's goals were to reduce the incidence of situations manifesting destructive interactions in communication patterns with clients, and to reinforce the sense of synergy between the client and the merged company. This was critical in light of the fact that the new reality following the merger, being the feeling of lost personal service, required improving interactions with clients.

The road to improved service led to brainstorming meetings, in which managers and employees of both companies participated. There, the areas of responsibility were more sharply focused, and a work plan for improved service was defined. A joint workshop was also held for company representatives and clients, seeking to ease the clients' coping with the post-merger interactions while hearing ideas on how to relate to the changes.

The goal we seek must be defined and clear so that all employees in all divisions will understand it, connect with it and adopt it.

I recommend defining this goal or purpose, as far as possible, in a way that allows it to be measured. For example, instead of setting a somewhat abstract purpose of "merging the two sales departments in the organization," the goal needs to be more fully detailed as "merging the two sales departments into one, so that within six months all salespersons from both pre-merger departments will be capable of selling all products provided by the organization."

Instead of saying, for example, that "our objective is to improve the service offered by the organization," quantify that goal: "Our objective is to achieve improvement in the index for satisfaction in at least two areas within a year." At least the framework of time for reaching the new synergistic reality should be defined in clear measurable detail.

At this point, all aspects of synergy should be addressed in reference to their importance for the organizational reality. I would recommend taking another look at the list of aspects in Chapter 2, page 65.

◑ What resources are needed for achieving this purpose?

Having defined the objective you want to reach, you now need to examine the resources required for executing that change. Examine three types of resources: internal, external, and supporting processes.

◎ Internal resources

Leadership and commitment. This is component 2, noted above, for successful assimilation. First, ensure that the organization has leaders who are committed to the process and involved in the planning stage. This is a critical resource for successfully creating synergy. As the person responsible for the synergy process, you need to check whether this level of commitment exists, and if not, try to create it. You also need to define who will lead the change: the CEO, the VP, or another senior manager.

Steering committee / change management team. The synergy process requires resources from various units in the organization, which is why I recommend establishing a steering committee, headed by the person who leads the process, liaise among units, guide them, assist the change leader, and recruit resources in favor of the process. This is the framework in which all involved can join in and express their various views.

Resources of time and funds. Estimate what the cost of creating the new reality would be, how much funding is needed to implement it, and whether that sum is available to the organization. Check also whether there is sufficient time to execute the process.

The full synergy assimilation process is lengthy, starting from the stage of defining the new reality up to the stage where employees feel comfortable in their ongoing work based on these new interactions; this is why it is so important to plan and ensure that resources are available.

For example, if you appoint a steering committee, you need to ensure that its members are allocated sufficient time to implement necessary actions, and ensure that meetings are held on work time and not on their private time. This means defining designated windows of time in advance, such as two hours per week, or twice a month, to be wholly devoted to steering committee meetings.

Despite limited resources of time and money, you can nonetheless embed the synergy form quickly and effectively by using the work process, tools and especially, the questionnaire presented at the end of Chapter 2, and create that new reality. Assimilating the synergy form contributes significantly to increasing the organization's outputs over time.

External resources

Sometimes, creating a new reality requires recruiting external resources: inputs which the organization needs in order to achieve the new reality, but currently does not have. Check which external resources will be needed for the process: are they readily available, and in sufficient quantities? Think about the physical and intellectual resources, such as organizational knowhow, technological knowledge, legal or accounting resources, which are not inside the organization. Take into account that intellectual resources must remain in the organization at the end of the process, and not disappear when the consultant's role has been completed.

Supporting processes

Supporting processes are an internal resource which aims to improve effectiveness and efficiency in the organization. At this stage, examine whether processes already exist in your organization that can support the synergy assimilation process: what can you already use, and what would need to undergo change in order to become an effective supporting process?

For example: a common supporting process is decision making. If this is conducted hierarchically in your organization, I would recommend instituting a new decision-making process or procedure which requires making decisions jointly with all those involved in the matter. In the same way, you could examine the processes for time management, and management of meetings: do they exist in your organization, and can they be made to serve the synergy assimilation process?

Other supporting processes involve management of human resources: training, workshops, development meetings, remunerations systems (as mentioned in components 8 and 9 above), and employee evaluation. It is worth examining how you can make use of these processes to have employees and managers join in the synergy assimilation process and create the new reality you seek to promote. This enables you to make the new language and its advantages familiar to them, recruit their support, expand their involvement, and link them to the synergy approach and the new reality's formulation, by making them feel not only that they are part of it but that they identify with it. Identification on the part of employees helps reduce resistance or opposition to the change.

Case Study

Working with a small company in the field of PR which sought to improve interactions, the issue of distributing the annual holiday bonus came up. I was informed that part of the company's remuneration system included a customary monetary bonus to its 40 employees.

The previous year, employees had received bonuses based

solely on the proprietors' considerations. This caused bitterness among many of them, who felt that the decision was unfair and experienced it as invasive in synergy terms.

This being a small company, my suggestion was to examine, together with the employees, what gave rise to these sensations, and what the best way would be to remunerate them: whether through a single annual bonus or a fixed increase to their salaries, remuneration should be set based on the quality of the employee's performance in the previous year and no other consideration.

I was very pleased when the proprietors agreed to this change, and about half the employees chose to have the bonus integrated into their salaries. This case shows how supporting processes which involve employees contribute to synergy and a new reality: employees received a chance to express their difference while being remunerated. Their satisfaction rose, the sense of unfairness dropped significantly, and in general, their opposition to the synergy assimilation process was reduced.

In any event, it is important to stress that the responsibility for the synergy assimilation process remains with the organization, as does the unique knowledge accrued, and that the organization is the entity which must continue preserving and reinforcing this new culture.

2. The in-depth diagnostic stage

Once you've completed the planning stage and reviewed the resources within your organization, it's time to diagnose the existing situation from the perspective of interactions, and characterize your point of reference, which is the status you want to achieve. This stage is carried out using the questionnaire presented in Chapter 2. Where needed, you can integrate personal interviews.

It's very important that the questionnaire is handled by a consultant or a manager trained for this purpose, who will accompany the process. From my experience, even though the questionnaire is well structured and contains clear instructions, questions always arise about how to fill it in.

The questionnaire is best passed around as part of a meeting or workshop, allowing the various types of interactions to be demonstrated, which links questionnaire responses to the process of developing the team.

A scenario of lesser value, but nonetheless possible, is to hand out questionnaires during a personal interview which you conduct with each person. The interviewee in this case receives maximum attention and all concerns about the questionnaire's nature and purpose can be addressed. This ensures that the individual can process some of the information personally without involving the group. However, it forgoes the benefits of receiving other important information that tends to surface in the context of dynamic group process. Handing out questionnaires as part of interviews is appropriate in an organization that is less open, where it is feared that participants may not express themselves freely in a workshop scenario.

In the questionnaire processing, or diagnostic, stage, it is important to note who filled the questionnaire in, and to whom that individual is referring, as well as the general picture which emerges. Although throughout the book I've emphasized that the mix of forms is subjective, it's still very important to note if a recurring form shows up within a particular unit or group. You can calculate the average points which each person has applied to every form of interaction, dividing the total points by the number of participants, either at the team, unit or whole organization level.

But beyond the statistical calculations it's no less important to pay close attention to examples that employees provide. These can clearly indicate the real-time status in your organization at the level of individual, group, or the whole organization. If necessary, reread Chapter 2, paying special attention to the issue of subjectivity for each form versus the option of conducting an in-depth analysis at the organizational and team levels.

The questionnaire in Chapter 2 reflects the overall framework, but when working with a specific organization, I prepare a unique questionnaire which takes into account that organization's needs. In many instances the questionnaire will focus on a topic chosen by the organization's management, such as staff and line interactions or improved service, rather than asking employees what topic they prefer to work on (Question 1).

In general we could say that in every organization, we want to reach a state where the forms of invasion or obscurity will be less than 5% of interactions. Simultaneously, we aim for synergy to become one of the organization's dominant forms, and that the three quality forms: interdependence, interfaced, and synergy will account for at least 70% of the total.

In addition to the questionnaire, other diagnostic tools are used in processes of organizational development, such as appreciative inquiry, an approach that emphasizes the organization's strengths rather than weaknesses.

Having completed the diagnosis and received a picture of things as they stand as far as current interactions in the organization, the next stage requires defining the status we aim for as a benchmark, characterizing areas where particular problems occur, and topics that need focusing on.

At the close of the diagnostic stage we take a look at the findings and prepare the work plan agreed on by management, adapting it with maximum precision to the needs which have surfaced. The work plan must include milestones, landmarks for the work process, division of areas of responsibility, and a review of resources available to the organization.

3. The change implementation stage

The stage in which change is implemented involves applying all the recommendations for improving interactions in the organization, as discussed in previous chapters and in the review of components for successfully assimilating the synergy process. Expanded information on ways to improve this appears in Chapter 4. It is important to note that the steering committee should continue to accompany the process, beyond the planning stage.

From my experience, at this stage appointing improvement teams is critical. Improvement teams help execute real-time adaptations and adjustments, reduce expression of destructive forms, strengthen the ability of employees to accept diversity among themselves, and make communication among departments or people more efficient. These teams can also adapt work procedures to the new needs, and in many other ways, execute real time improvements. Documenting the improvement teams' work ensures that the knowledge they accrue stays in the organization long after the consultant, if one has been hired, goes home.

Case Study

My work involves helping set up a great many improvement teams in diverse organizations. One of these was an advertising and public relations organization. It had a fairly compartmentalized structure, with a relatively large number of employees also doubling as client portfolio holders, each working with specific clients. For various reasons, it was valuable to improve the synergy among the employees, and between employees and the company's management.

The company had no dedicated unit for human resources or training functions. We decided to establish a human resources and social services improvement team, which worked for a fairly long period directly with the CEO to bring about significant improvements on areas of social service, employee selection, employee recruitment, remuneration, and more. The team was allocated an annual budget. As a result of its efforts, the quality of handling the organization's human capital rose, matched by an increase in satisfaction. Other organizational aspects, such as successful recruitment of employees, also improved. In this way, without financing an expensive human resources function,

> we managed to bring about the improvements through synergistic actions of a relatively small number of employees and managers in the company.
>
> In another company, improvement teams operated, with good results in areas closer to the functional core, such as work processes, reducing bottlenecks, secretarial services for company employees, and more.

Several points which assist activating improvement teams:

◉ The teams' work must be voluntary. It is not productive to force an employee to participate in an improvement team.

◉ Activities must take place during regular work hours.

◉ Improvement teams should receive appropriate authority to act, and a budget for their task.

◉ In striving to assimilate synergy in the organization, improvement teams must be completely familiar with all issues in the field.

◉ Members of improvement teams must hold roles from a diverse array of levels in the organization.

At this point I want to relate briefly to one of the differences between improvement teams in small organizations, compared to large organizations.

In most small organizations numbering several dozen employees, usually no one has been entrusted with the function of executing organizational changes, such as the HR manager, an organizational development manager, a training manager, a procedures and methods manager, and so on. My experience shows that in small organizations, there is value in creating a team that takes on issues related to improvement and executes changes in addition to the participating employees' formal functions. The objective is to find employees who are interested in, and drawn to, activities relevant to an improvement team, or who want to use the opportunity to prove their professional capability as a basis for being promoted, or for personal gratification.

By contrast, in large organizations we usually find a department entrusted with all the functions for effecting organizational change, on one hand, and lateral HQ work, on the other. Having a designated organizational unit makes it easier to start the process of improving interactions. However, working according to fixed procedures, organized work norms and organizational politics may contribute to creating rigid boundaries, which do not make it easy to introduce cultural changes or embed the synergy process.

4. The change assimilation stage

If you want to ensure that the synergy approach is preserved in your organization, devote attention to embedding it into your ongoing management. You can do this by integrating changes in the supporting processes, as recommended in the discussion of the planning stage: that is, primarily in decision making, coordination, remuneration, training, and managers development.

You can distribute the diagnostic questionnaire annually as a means of examining and characterizing trends and processes in the organization. This allows you to track the distribution of percentages for the different patterns on an annual basis, and use the data for manager development training and workshops.

In any case, whether you are personally responsible for having the synergy approach assimilated in your organization, or that is achieved through the services of a hired external consultant, it is vital to ensure that the knowledge stays with your organization, and to allocate suitable resources for assimilating it. Too many organizations are not conscientious in that regard, and for various reasons seem to tire before reaching this stage. Sometimes the budget has run out, or the defined time frame has ended, but this means that any gains made until that point, most likely with hard work by many, are simply lost. Be sure at the planning stage to allocate resources for every stage, and avoid excesses that do not serve your purpose.

5. Change evaluation and QA

Once the change is made and assimilation has been implemented, the next stage involves measuring and controlling it. This is when you check whether the goal has been achieved: did you successfully reach the target of quality interactions in the organization, and are these quality interactions appearing in the desirable range of percentages?

As already noted, one of the correct ways for undertaking evaluation and control is through redistributing the 7 Forms of Interaction questionnaire and / or through cross-section interviews with employees. If you choose to distribute the questionnaire again, be as careful with instructions and explanations the second time around as you were the first time.

6. Repeating the process until the target is achieved

If you have not achieved your target, it may need to be altered or redefined. In other words, we need to repeat the second stage and re-determine the point of reference, and / or introduce additional improvements into the process, until the desired outcome is reached. This is the essence of the sixth stage.

Summary and Your Personal Workbook

This chapter has reviewed the components and stages for successfully assimilating the synergy process. I hope you've already completed the personal summary table as the chapter has moved forward. I recommend that you now write down all the remarks and points relating to each stage, relative to your organization's characteristics and the specific reality you want to create. View this activity as a simulation before starting out on actual implementation.

1. Initial diagnosis and plan

_____

_____

_____

_____

_____

2. In-depth diagnosis stage

_____

_____

_____

_____

_____

3. Change implementation stage

_____

_____

_____

_____

_____

4. Change assimilation stage

5. Change evaluation and QA stage

6. Process repeat as needed

CHAPTER 4
Synergy or Wasted Energy: Rules and tips for improving interactions

This chapter provides effective and practical rules and tips that will help you upgrade your ability to independently manage the synergy improvement process in your organization. The examples included show how to manage the organization correctly, based on the synergy approach.
The following sections in this chapter include workbook pages and space at the end of each section, for writing down your remarks.

Synergy is a language. Learn it! It covers how to think, how to speak, and how to behave, synergistically.

- ⦿ **How to correctly manage diversity**
- ⦿ **How to correctly manage boundaries**
- ⦿ **How to correctly manage communication: techniques for improving communication in the organization**
- ⦿ **How to correctly manage interactions**

As with any language, the language of synergy needs to be taught, learned, and practiced. This is why I recommend that you become the first one to practice it while reading this book: in other words, read this book with your pen at hand for entering remarks, because this is definitely a book meant for study. Jot down notes in the margins, underline key points, use colored markers. Do whatever works for you. You'll find that this makes practicing the language of synergy much easier when you reread the sections and come across the notes of significance for you and your organization, and the change it is experiencing.

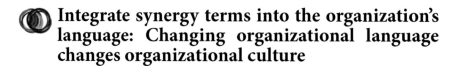 ## Integrate synergy terms into the organization's language: Changing organizational language changes organizational culture

Use the terms from the language of synergy and integrate them into your organization's language. When I work with organizations, I use concepts such as "purple," which describes the interface between red and blue; "diversity," "organizational synergy," "flexible boundaries," "blurring," and "invasion," and maintain each one's unique meaning relative to the synergy approach. I integrate them into my speech, so that employees practice "synergistic thinking," get accustomed to it, and behave accordingly.

The more you practice the synergy approach, the more you'll find yourself using more positive, respectful, enabling and containing language. Criticisms which arouse divisiveness, rigidify boundaries, create distance, and emphasize ego will be replaced by expressions that enhance team work and connecting with other members of the organization. The overall cultural mood will be based on listening, dialogue, and partnership in problem solving.

Share what's happening with your employees

Bring your employees in on events and inform them of processes about to occur in the organization. I'm frequently asked when, how and whether it's right to involve employees in changes the organization is seeking to implement. Often, especially when a merger or acquisition is about to happen, the controlling party and managers are very concerned about sharing the situation with employees, fearing that this may injure the process.

I can't guarantee that sharing information with employees

will not cause them to have doubts, and their doubts certainly have understandable grounds, which I respect. However, my recommendation is that, in most cases, there is value in informing employees of impending changes as soon as there is no danger of causing harm to your organization's financial or commercial interests.

You can share with employees in the context of a joint meeting or workshop, or an authorized party can convey the necessary information to all relevant persons while offering an opportunity for involvement. Another alternative is to convey the information using the fanning out method, where senior management informs intermediate management, which in turn informs employees. In extremely large organizations, tools are usually in place for internal communication. I recommend not having such changes suddenly land on the employees' laps: this will not be perceived as partnership but as one-way communication or even as invasion.

Case Study

Some years ago I was invited to work with a company involved in transportation. The company was undergoing major change, switching from government to private ownership. To my surprise, a very untypical event for the culture in which the company operated occurred at the outset, when the VP of HR invited the head of the workers' union to participate in the meetings, starting from the very first one which discussed, among other issues, the planned change processes in terms of how and when. I was favorably surprised, and discovered that this mode of action, and later involvement of employees themselves in the process, greatly assisted in implementing the necessary changes.

An important rule of thumb in employee collaboration is never to make assumptions concerning their attitudes or feelings, or how they experience your organization's various boundaries, communication patterns, and diversity. It's far better to ask questions and be clear, as far as possible, than to make assumptions which tend to be based on rumor and may lead to undesirable outcomes.

Never assume! Always check with the source!

Use your sound logic: make use of the interactions questionnaire to check what employees and managers really think and feel.

Yes, in actuality we do need to make some assumptions because reality is complex and we can't examine every fine detail. However, assumptions cause mistakes. The most common of these is: If I feel we have good interactions, I assume you must feel the same way. This assumption emphasizes just how subjectively interactions are perceived, and how wide the gap can be between aspiring to synergy and your employees' authentic experience of these interactions.

Even if management makes clear statements and shows by personal example how to behave in the organization based on the synergy approach, it isn't enough. People continue functioning based on their own sensations, interpretations and how they are affected by the change. This is what makes collaboration so critical to success.

Summary and your personal workbook

Synergy is a language. Learn it: how to think, speak and behave synergistically.

_____

_____

_____

What will you start doing tomorrow? What do you plan for the longer term?

_____

_____

_____

How to correctly manage diversity

We've discussed diversity, and its importance as the basis for creating synergy. Below are several valuable suggestions for correctly managing diversity in the organization, but beforehand, a real-time event...

Case Study

One of the occasions when I was personally exposed to intercultural diversity occurred during a teaching stint at Assumption University, Thailand. The Thai culture is very different from the Western culture I grew up in and predominantly work with, and this experience allowed me to learn how strongly cultural diversity affects an organization's interactions.

In classroom teaching during the semester, the boundaries between students and me were rigid, making it harder for me to bridge the gaps between us and create synergy in the learning process. One of the first phenomena I encountered was linked to a seemingly simple and trivial matter: responses to emails I sent to university staff while preparing for the trip, and to students at the start of studies. I wasn't always responded to, which I found very odd. At the personal level, I perceived it as a lack of good manners.

I later learned that saying "no" was strongly avoided in the local culture. If I asked a colleague or student a specific question which they would need to answer with a "no,", or if a student was not sure about how to answer a question or perhaps felt uncomfortable with the question, the preferred option was simply not to answer.

Language was another obstacle in creating synergy between the students and me. Even though this was an international university and its official language was English, the predominantly Thai students complained about their difficulty in understanding my accent, just as it was difficult for me to understand theirs.

Another situation I clearly recall took place during a break between classes. I was talking to a student who described his experiences as an officer in the Thai military. Pleased with his sharing, I also shared the fact that I had been a military officer. Immediately he went silent, as though embarrassed or perhaps threatened. Bottom line, this conversation created a more rigid barrier between us.

Even before reaching Thailand, I knew that cultural diversity would need to be bridged. I was unaware of just how vast the gap was, but my wish to create dialogue with the students and overcome the cultural disparities was honest and authentic. This led me to adopting several actions. In our first class, I gave every student a small gift which I'd brought with me: a small cross made of olive wood. This token was received warmly by the students, especially the Christians among them. During the semester, I made sure to eat lunch in the dining hall with students, each time with a different group, which helped me make the very formal classroom relationship somewhat more flexible.

I also placed importance on holding personal meetings with the students, beyond the formal classroom hours or official office times. I invited them to the teaching staff's residences lobby, where the atmosphere was more easy-going. In classes I used simulation and role play, and made sure that detailed presentations were made in each class, so that students could read the material and not rely only on listening, which helped them overcome the problem of our different accents. And for this same reason, I asked them to write their answers on the board rather than say them out loud. In general, I invested a good deal of effort in connecting with the local faculty and administration, going out with them in our free time, joining their weekend trips and so on, rather than keeping to myself.

And it appeared that these actions did make boundaries more flexible. In the students' final project, they prepared skits and clips. The atmosphere was far less formal than it had been at the semester's outset.

Being respectful does not mean having to agree

Successful coping with diversity in the organization requires respectfulness towards the other person's diversity, understanding it by learning about its sources, its characteristics and its dimensions. But this scope of familiarization does not require agreement, or disagreement, with what that person does or says.

I frequently encounter the incorrect perception among an organization's staff, that being respectful to someone who has a different opinion to mine means agreeing with that person. Even if not explicitly stated, this perception subconsciously impacts the organization's interactions, such as when one person does not agree with another and is therefore not interested in conducting any communication with the other and respecting the other's stance. Nonetheless, manifestations of coexistence, or attempts at finding platforms for coexistence, can often be found, as the following incident describes.

Case Study

The difficulty in acknowledging and respecting the other's diversity was clearly evident when I facilitated a project promoting coexistence between Jewish and Arab students in Haifa University's School of Political Science.

My first obstacle was to be perceived as a neutral entity instead of an Israeli Jewish one. It was hard for students to understand, accept and respect my neutral stance. For a lengthy period we tried to overcome the commonplace outlooks associated with each of the two groups, implement a synergy approach, and acknowledge that it is possible to accept the other without necessarily agreeing to the other's opinions.

Two main actions contributed to achieving acceptance and respect:

1. To start with, I felt it would be correct to invite a consultant from the Arab sector to facilitate the project in collaboration with me. Starting with the second year, a female Arab consultant working with the methodology of listening circles, which will be presented further on, joined me. The mode of shared facilitation demonstrated to students that coexistence in the microcosm is achievable, which made it easier for students to create synergy among themselves. This example also shows how important it is for organizational consultants and group facilitators to be personal role models, implementing synergy as far as possible within, or despite, the framework of limited possibilities and resources available to them as they teach processes.

> 2. In each study series, we renewed our agreement that although we may not agree on the substance, we nevertheless agreed to create a "bubble" of agreement: every team agreed to promote its project without any linkage to what was happening in the external world.

This example serves to demonstrate the ability to work together even in situations of a lack of chemistry between cultures, and instead, focus on the importance of the topic, or the shared goal at hand, in this case completion of the program's final project, and achieving the students' wish for better acquaintance across groups.

Eventually the students found a way to successfully flex their boundaries. Among the actions they took were visiting each other at home, enjoying shared meals, holding informal conversations, and primarily learning to acknowledge and respect the other as an individual, as someone with a family, hobbies, and so on, all of which greatly helped improve interactions among them. Further into this chapter, under the heading "How to correctly manage boundaries", we'll discuss the "synergy bubble" in more detail.

Creating a discourse on diversity in your organization

Discussing diversity helps managers and employees in your organization understand just how dominant diversity is in our lives. In any conversation on diversity, I recommend starting out with an activity, such as the massage exercise presented below. This can be followed by asking participants to offer examples of aspects of diversity, and asking them questions that arouse discussion about the nature and contribution of these aspects to interactions in the organization. Choose an aspect that arouses difficulty or conflict, and offer a more in-depth explanation about its impact on organizational interactions.

The massage exercise

As noted, I tend to use this exercise in organizations as part of synergy training. Its purpose is to demonstrate the experience of diversity to participants and arouse discussion. This exercise is conducted at the start of the workshop, to break the ice among participants, with the discussion on diversity held only afterwards. If you want to use this activity in your organization, be sure to follow the instructions carefully, and not offer any advance explanation regarding the activity's purpose.

To conduct this activity, have participants stand in a circle, one behind the other, so that every participant can massage the person in front of her or him at that point where the neck and shoulders meet. This spot is often stiff, and causes some pain when worked on.

Participants must not talk to each other during the exercise. They are only allowed to identify the other person's body language, and through non-verbal communication, receive permission to massage the person in front. No words, none at all. Eye contact is the only way to receive or grant permission, or rejection, to massage. This means each person must make eye contact with 2 people, the one in front, and the one behind.

As an ice-breaker, it goes like this: (1) Ask participants to stand in a circle (2) Ask them to turn so that they are now one behind the other (3) Explain that each person will massage the shoulders of the person in front, and that no speaking is allowed, only non-verbal language for requesting and receiving permission to massage (4) Allocate 2 minutes for the activity from this point on (5) Discussion and summary.

To close the activity, I ask participants why they think I opened the workshop with it. I'm surprised to see how frequently insights on diversity surface, such as where the boundary lies between pleasant or embarrassing, with whom it's comfortable to work and with whom less so, and whether a massage from a person of a particular gender is embarrassing.

Often, at least one participant refuses to join in the exercise. I allow this, but make sure that in the group discussion which follows, the person's choice is referred to, discussing why this choice might be made, as well as how it links to diversity and boundaries. Humor is the best way of coping with any tension or embarrassment that may arise. Participants often use laughter and joking as a way of overcoming any awkwardness surfacing from the exercise, either as an outcome of the physical contact, or the interaction with others.

If you decide to do this exercise in your organization, I suggest asking participants not only the questions noted above, but several additional ones: To what degree was the physical contact annoying or pleasant? Were there moments when it was more comfortable, or less so? What is each person's boundary relative to physical contact? Does physical contact with a colleague or other employee make them feel uncomfortable? Does physical contact with a senior manager, or subordinate, cause discomfort? Does anyone think the exercise involved penetration of personal space?

The insights offered in response to these questions help participants understand just how dominant diversity is in our lives. In one brief simple activity, we successfully raise various aspects and angles of diversity. I also suggest explaining to participants that the exercise manifested the flexible boundaries between the person giving the massage and the person being massaged, which allows creating, even for those few moments, the experience of a new reality in the workplace.

Please not that this exercise is not suitable for every culture.

The discourse on diversity

Having broken the ice, participants are usually more at ease and willing to hold a discussion on diversity in their organization. Initially, to get the discussion up and running, ask participants to offer examples of diversity in the organization: you can link specialization and diversity, noting that various employees have different professions. This type of diversity is clear and familiar, and doesn't come across as threatening.

The goal is to help participants bring other examples of a more threatening or focused nature to the surface. These may relate to gender, ethnicity, nationality, physical or other impairment, strengths or weaknesses. Ask participants which aspects, in their view, arouse more conflict or difficulty in the organization's daily functioning, and why.

Once the 'problematic' aspects have been aired, ask participants to consider how each aspect may contribute value to the organization: for example, a balance between people who make their decisions rationally, compared to those who make emotion-based decisions, allows the organization a reality that takes into account employees' needs while operating on the basis of economic considerations. A balance between an optimistic outlook and a pessimistic one, or as pessimists like to term it, an informed realistic viewpoint, can bring about innovation and simultaneously avoid a serious fall.

Here is the order of questions for the discussion:
1. Present examples showing aspects of diversity in the organization.
2. Which aspect, in your view, causes conflict or difficulty at work, and why?
3. What does each aspect contribute to the organization?

The final stage, once the discussion has calmed down and everyone has stated their opinion, is to expand on one of the aspects. If you're closely familiar with the organization, you can prepare a discussion topic in advance.

One example for extended discussion: The difference in management style between men and women.

The difference between men and women is perhaps the most common area of discussion: this diversity is clear, dominant, evident, and manifests both in the workplace and outside it. Acknowledging the diversity in management styles between men and women, and respecting both styles, is the basis for creating a synergistic organizational administration. By contrast, when administration is too homogenous, blind spots develop, which can cause built-in breakdowns in the organization.

It is important to stress that every manager, irrespective of gender, uses both masculine and feminine styles of management, but the balance will be different. A masculine management style tends to rationally based actions, which suppress emotion and fears. This makes it harder to flex boundaries, and unresolved areas may continue to ferment beneath the surface. If these unresolved areas are not clearly and assertively expressed in open dialogue, they will become embodied in conflicts or patterns of invasion, which makes creating synergy so much harder. By contrast, the feminine management style tends to give greater expression to emotion both in ongoing work and in decision making processes, which allows greater opportunity for creating synergy. However, the tendency to avoid entering conflicts, more typical of feminine management style, can cause blurring when defining boundaries.

From my experience, men tend to invade more than women, and women identify men as more invasive, but this does not imply that the masculine management style will not allow for synergy. It's definitely possible, as long as we stay aware of the inhibiting factors in this management style, and work to respectfully acknowledge the contribution of each gender's style to the organization.

Any organization in a process of creating synergy, and any manager seeking to lead this move, must allow both management styles to coexist, rather than force women to adopt a masculine management style, an approach that unfortunately can still be found in some organizational cultures. The organization should allow "working from the head" alongside "working from the heart", and understand that true synergy is based on both together.

Lastly, you may want to close the discussion by requesting participants for feedback and conclusions.

Learn to live with diversity by viewing it as a challenge, not a threat

Since our perception of interactions is always subjective, when a manager or employee experiences invasion there's no point in offering "objective" or rational explanations of why that perception is incorrect. Accepting that the person's feeling is subjective is the first step in handling it. It's important to remember that any action which encourages synergy contributes to promoting flexible boundaries, and flexible boundaries in turn encourage synergy. A different perception of reality therefore doesn't have to be viewed as a threat. It should be related to as a challenge, as described in the situation below.

Case Study

In one of the organizations I worked with, I focused for a lengthy period on working with the development department, which was managed by a very aggressive Development VP. As part of the synergy creation and interaction improvement process, I handed the 7 forms of interaction questionnaire out to employees. Analyzing the responses, I found a wide range of differences for obscurity and invasion: some employees reported high levels of up to 25% in both, whereas others reported very low levels of these two forms.

The Development VP, like so many managers of this type, did not respect the employees' subjective sensations, and instead of allowing this range among the department's employees to manifest, he used the findings from employees who did not report blurring to "prove" that obscurity didn't really exist. That only added fuel to the fire!

In this case, I conducted an advance process with the manager, in order to avoid criticism of the VP in front of the department's employees during their joint workshop. The proceedings were not simple, but after several personal meetings, a turning point was reached, whereby the VP was willing to acknowledge the diversity in his department, and handle each situation individually as raised by those employees who reported high levels of obscurity and invasion. We then went back to collaborative workshop activities for creating synergy among all the department's employees.

Summary and your personal workbook

How can diversity be correctly managed? What will you do tomorrow, and what will you handle in the longer term relative to the following points?

Being respectful doesn't mean having to agree - remark

_____

_____

_____

Set up a discussion on diversity

_____

_____

_____

Learn to live with diversity by viewing it as a challenge, not a threat

_____

_____

_____

How to handle boundaries correctly

Correct handling of boundaries in your organization is critical to improving interactions and creating synergy. My experience shows, however, that dealing with the axis of boundaries is less clear to managers and consultants. This is why I believe it's beneficial to relate to this area from several different but complementary angles.

Correct use of job descriptions

One of the predominant characteristics of post-modern organizations is how frequently they change. In turn, this causes the boundaries for various employees to change, which routinely leads to blurring. Clear and rigid job definitions was a twentieth century characteristic, but many organizations still use job descriptions as a way of marking, and even rigidifying, boundaries among the organization's employees.

Recently, however, I increasingly hear the claim that there is currently no need for job descriptions, since most positions in the organization change at very high rates, and it's impossible to constantly keep updating the descriptions. Additionally, in some cases job descriptions may cause damage, because they set very limited work norms when in fact greater professional and cognitive flexibility is needed.

Managers who recognize this need tend to encourage states of blurred boundaries, claiming that a certain degree of obscurity enables flexibility and allows them to ask, or require, an employee to do whatever the manager needs or wants, without having to give too much thought to the strict definition, or boundary, of that employee's position.

My experience shows that it is always worthwhile to maintain a formal job definition, which allows coordinating expectations, and prevents obscurity. When I write up job descriptions for organizations, I stress the need for flexibility and team work, and define the critical partners for executing the particular role, which inherently defines the synergy between them. In this way I can link the job analysis to the team development process: in other words, I relate concurrently to the role, its relationship to the team function, and the individual filling it.

If at this point you're feeling confused, you may not yet have assimilated the distinction between flexibility and blurring.

Flexible boundaries are definitely a positive condition, which contributes to creating synergy. Blurring, however, indicates organizational illness which needs treatment. Once again, I remind you that we're discussing perceptions, and it's important to ensure that the perceived level of blurring does not rise above 7%.

Case Study

At the start of my professional career, I headed a military job description unit. At the time, precise role definitions, or "classic" activity analyses, as I call them these days, were a common tool for creating organizational order. But they limited the role filler to one specific area and allowed no room for deviation, much like workers in a manufacturing plant who endlessly repeat the same action on the assembly line.

One of the more interesting findings surfacing from my Master's thesis, which dealt with enriching the jobs for soldiers in compulsory military service, was that in certain circumstances, this very rigidity in defining the role led to distortions and in retrospect, made it harder to achieve synergy among the team: for example, between officers and cadets, or among cadets in similar positions. The outcome was a feeling of heavy burden on the part of those filling one role, usually officers involved in a tough but challenging position, compared to sense of boredom and lack of room to maneuver felt by those in the other role, usually the cadets

At a later stage in my career, I was involved in a project which aimed to develop and train technicians, particularly in the field of electronics, since the rigid job definition made it more difficult to find suitable individuals. The new organizational reality required a more flexible analysis of roles that would allow more teamwork and less need for specific experts. Following the project, several retraining programs were instituted, some of which remain active to date: a program for retraining primarily female soldiers with high school science backgrounds for technological positions; a program to transfer tasks from officers and engineers to enlisted non-academic military personnel; and a program to expand integration of women in an array of roles

Currently when I prepare job analyses for various functions in organizations, I devote far more attention to collaborators in any role, and how they may communicate and uphold effective interactions, and focus less on precision definitions of that role's tasks.

Creating a "synergy bubble"

As a manager you might need to cope with extreme situations which may require shielding the organization's staff from the external world, and creating an artificial bubble in which synergy can be achieved. These kinds of situations may occur when the organization contains groups of different nationalities or sociological backgrounds, when the external environment is highly conflictual and highlights diversity in a way that is hard to cope with, or when the employee has no clear personal interest in collaboration, such as when the employee knows she or he is about to be dismissed and develops a hostile attitude.

As noted in the case history on page 123, which describes my work with binational teams of students from the Jewish and the Arab sectors, the Arab students found it very difficult to disconnect from their harsh feelings concerning their Jewish co-students, who represented from their viewpoint what they called "the Zionist occupation," and move towards shaping some level of dialogue. The synergy bubble was presented as a neutral space where collaborative teams were asked to relate wholly and solely to the current synergistic space and the set goals or tasks that needed to be performed.

To encourage collaboration within the "synergy bubble," I recommend rewarding team members for upholding targets and achieving the goals defined for them. Each organization can find the right way to recognize these achievements; and recognition doesn't necessarily have to be monetary.

Clarifying boundaries

The more that blurred boundaries are perceived as a norm in your organization, the more it's worth dealing with this area so that you can enjoy the advantages of the synergy approach. If questionnaires come back showing that in more than 7% of the interactions blurring has ben reported an action is required. Many organizations tend to clarify boundaries through their job descriptions, but this technique is not appropriate if the employees themselves are not involved in defining their jobs. If you conduct a role definition process without employee agreement, you may cause an increase in the sense of invasion, or no interaction, which is more destructive than blurring. In any event, you can overcome blurring by defining boundaries through direct and open dialogue with each person involved.

Use your sound logic to differentiate between flexible boundaries and blurred boundaries

At the start of the section on diversity, I presented the example of the VP of Development who found difficulty in accepting the sensations of obscurity and invasion which many of his team's members reported in the " 7 Forms of Interaction" questionnaire. When I presented the data to him, he initially tried to justify the situation with an explanation: "Obscurity helps me. We're a small department, and each technician has to cover numerous functions. I'm comfortable when I can ask any technician to do what I need at that moment."

This wasn't new to me. I'd heard it repeatedly from many managers, it is hard to invalidate, and trying to do that may actually be incorrect. But it's worth keeping in mind that the sensation of blurring, like any other form, is subjective. Employees who identify and define the nature of their work in this manager's department as having a high level of blurring are actually saying "I've got a problem here," and over time, if the problem is not resolved, it turns into invasion conflict.

There is great value in preventing this from happening, even when the reality in which the organization operates frequently changes. Agreement should be reached on the role's definition: what it includes, and what parts of it can, or should, be flexible. This is the only way to reduce the sensation of blurring. I'd suggest that as a manager, you should use your sound logic and familiarization with the organization and its employees on one hand, and input from the questionnaires on the other, to prevent blurring and instead, preserve and reinforce flexibility in defining boundaries.

Flexing boundaries

Preventing blurring is vital for creating quality forms of interaction in the organization and especially, synergy, but that's not enough. Boundaries need to be made flexible. Keep in mind that if more than 7% blurring is reported, boundaries first need to be defined before you can work on making them flexible.

Most people have difficulty in creating flexible boundaries, because they don't feel sufficiently comfortable or sure of themselves vis-à-vis a flexible boundary. Open work spaces, for example, are experienced as spaces which lack boundaries, and force employees to give consideration to other employees and accept their behavior. The more employees feel threatened, the more they will want to rigidify any flexible boundaries.

Should the European Union, for example, feel that European residents' personal safety was being undermined by open borders, it would tend to rigidify them again in certain locations, demand passport checks, and so on. At the time of this book's writing, for example, in November 2015, a terror attack was carried out in Paris. As a result, the French President announced a state of emergency that same evening, which included closing France's borders and all public areas, as well as grounding all planes in French airports until further notice.

The main tools for flexing boundaries among employees, and overcoming the difficulties noted above, are: infusing a sense of fairness, working transparently, and creating cooperation and involvement. These three tools are interlinked, and reinforce each other. Employees who feel that their employer or direct supervisor is fair towards them, and that any action affecting them is transparent, will become more involved. They'll feel far more protected and confident about flexing their boundaries. Improved communication (the second axis in the 7 Forms of Interaction Model), can also flex boundaries, as I explain further on.

By contrast, there is no value to transparency for employees if the system is perceived as unfair. Marginalization and keeping secrets from employees cause rigidified boundaries at best, and a sense of invasion at worst. And invasion is far more damaging than blurring.

Personal, and personality, traits and characteristics contribute to the differences in how the same boundaries are perceived by different people in the organizational. No single solution will suit all employees: any solution needs to be adapted to each specific employee. At the same time, you should avoid treating structural or cultural issues as though they are derived from the employee's character.

Case Study

I found very strong reactions to rigid boundaries in a manufacturing plant whose management hired me to work with them as they went through the process of buying another factory.

Shortly before I started my work, the organization had established a new department led by a professional manager brought in from outside the system expressly to fill this role. Despite the role's clear definition, this new manager's status in the organization was unlike that of other department managers, all of whom had 'grown up' in the concern and were invited to some board meetings. The new manager was excluded from board meetings.

Additionally, managers of the other departments conducted themselves as a closed clique. Among themselves, they maintained full transparency, a sense of involvement and responsibility towards the organization's success and even close personal friendships buttressed by joint football games every weekend. The new manager, on the other hand, was perceived as an 'external graft', and no attempt was made on their part to cooperate with him or create any closeness.

Even though it was abundantly clear that the new department was vital to the firm's prosperity and its successful foothold in a new, strategic niche, no effort was invested in clarifying or flexing boundaries between the new manager, and the rest of 'the crew,' who claimed the 'new guy' had a different character. As evidence, they cited that he was the only one describing 'problems.' The new manager, for his part, railed against the lack of collaboration, up to and even having his work sabotaged, and the administration's disregard and repudiation of salary conditions he'd been promised.

In the end, attempts at creating synergy in the organization failed, boundaries remained as they were, and the new manager was fired. The outcome was significant damage to the firm.

In many cases, multifaceted organizational interests, such as strategic, financial or marketing interests, prevent transparency and collaboration between management and employees, and cause marginalization and rigid boundaries. That is how the synergy paradox frequently manifests: decision-makers need to decide, based on risk versus benefit considerations, on the extent to which they can apply the principles of the synergy approach. The synergy paradox is described in detail in Chapter 2, and I recommend rereading this discussion, as it is very likely that you'll come across it in your organization.

Time is sometimes at the foundation to the solution: if the right method had been applied from the outset to minimize invasion and obscurity felt by employees, their confidence and trust would increase. That would make it easier to take actions which contradict the synergy approach when such steps are necessary. Those actions would be undertaken with the knowledge that the decision makers have their employees' and board's full backing to decide what is best for ensuring the organization's interests.

Once actions have been taken that reflect one-way decisions made by the organization's senior ranks, corrective measures can be implemented: explaining the considerations to employees; pointing out how not involving employees at the outset led to certain gains, if that is valid for the situation; and allowing employees to express their views or anger, and the feelings of obscurity or invasion they experienced during the period when no information was flowing down and they were kept out of the organization's decision making processes.

A typical example of this kind of situation is a firm that developed a unique technology but was about to be purchased by one of its clients due to lack of capital, and cash flow problems. The company's owners may have felt the need to conceal this information from employees and the board as a means of ensuring that the deal would go through safely. In retrospect, the purchase process, despite the obscurity or invasion it may have caused, led to saving the organization and possibly even higher salaries and benefits to employees. The company owners, nonetheless, had to cope with the synergy paradox: to consider how far the decision would harm interactions in the organization, and what rehabilitating steps would be needed later on.

We can go one step further to the example which runs through this book: it is impossible to force two people, even if they live together as a couple, to love each other. It's similarly impossible to force synergy between organizations, departments or teams against their members' wishes.

Unfortunately, I find too many examples of organizations and managers still trying to force synergy on their employees, which is a manifestation of coercion, and then finding it hard to understand why they fail. A typical attitude is, "They get their salaries. They should at least do what they're told." It is true: employees receive salaries for their work. But salaries don't assure motivation or involvement. And that leads to the next section. Please note that synergy can be created via the dimension of coercion and enforcement, yet it needs a goal that the workers appreciate.

Aspiring to satisfied employees

When we identity a pattern of blurring or rigid boundaries, we need to take into consideration that the patterns are perceived subjectively by each employee. This means that any defined boundary, no matter how precise and attuned to the reality, may not be acceptable to the person filling that role.

A manager's or employee's dissatisfaction with the definition of her or his role's boundaries may cause the role's boundaries to be disregarded, and may lead to feelings of obscurity and invasion between the employee and others in adjacent positions in the organization. Often, I come across statements by managers that "We ran a satisfaction survey and satisfaction was up." I'll emphasize that it is incorrect to base yourself on a data average, since the statistic could be misleading. Remember: one rotten apple in the barrel can ruin the barrel's entire contents; and the chain is only as strong as its weakest link. It can take no more than several dissatisfied employees, or sometimes just one, to cause significant damage to your organization.

In such cases, aim for an in-depth understanding of the reasons behind the employee's or manager's dissatisfaction, and try to improve the relationship. Beyond improved interactions between the individual employee and the organization, attending to the employee's personal difficulty conveys to other employees that the organization they work for is dependable and cares about them, which helps flex boundaries.

Applying changes that aim to improve embedding synergy in the organization requires cooperation on the part of the various interest holders, otherwise the entire process may be harmed, as the situation described below shows.

Case Study

Some years ago I was invited to advise an academic institution in assimilating a salary scale based on job descriptions.

At the outset of work, I was told that the management and the labor union agreed to start the process. However, as I started working, it quickly became clear that such an agreement did not exist. Worse yet, it was completely the opposite! Multiple differences of opinion came to light between the management and the union, raising difficulties and challenges that made completing the task close to impossible. These obstacles were primarily experienced by the management, which set rigid boundaries and was unwilling to cooperate in any meaningful way with the union representatives.

The management perceived embedding salary scales as being solely its prerogative, although it did agree to hold a joint discussion. Union representatives, on the other hand, viewed any attempt at influencing the salary structure as infringing on their rights, and as an invasion of its realm by the management, without honest collaboration.

This situation shows very clearly just how far disagreement on definitions of boundaries can go in causing the sense of invasion in the organization: employees, and primarily the union representatives, experienced the management actions as invasive and damaging to their interactions. None of this promotes synergy.

Yes, listen to your employees

We can sum up by saying that dealing with boundaries requires you to reduce expressions of blurring and rigidity as far as possible.

Boundaries are there to protect each of us, from the production floor all the way up to the CEO. We need to reach a state where every employee feels comfortable with the boundaries of her or his role, and her or his team.

Current organizational realities require adapting to changes and flexing boundaries. But frequent changes can cause a sensation of blurred and rigid boundaries: employees are asked to adapt themselves again and again to new situations, and their areas of responsibilities and authority are just as frequently expanded or reduced. Changes of this nature and frequency contribute to blurred boundaries, a sense of invasion, and insecurity among employees.

In situations of this kind we need to listen to employees, try our best to resolve their issues, and reduce their lack of clarity and / or feeling of threat as far as possible. It is important that the organization finds ways to acknowledge the personal diversity of its employees, and manifestations of this diversity in the organization. This is especially true, since the larger the organization, the more we tend to view employees in terms of groups and tag them with stereotypical labels. Learning and familiarizing with the topic can be integrated into development, training or facilitation processes for the future managerial pool, while at the same time reinforcing personal ties between employees and their direct supervisors, before the employee "disappears" into the team or the department.

The key to this is acknowledging the shades of difference among employees, respecting them, and giving a personal example of tolerance and admiration for each one's contribution. At the level of the direct manager as well as the whole organization we are committed to a culture of transparency, openness and involvement of employees relative to the organization's activities. Collaborative leadership ensures the existence of this organizational culture. In the next section, you will discover how communication assists in this goal, but first, a summary and personal practice workbook.

Summary and your personal workbook

How can boundaries be managed correctly? Write down whether you have identified situations in your organization that are similar to those described above. While you were reading, did you think of any solutions that you'd like to implement?

Correct usage of job descriptions

_____

_____

_____

_____

The synergy bubble: do you need to set up collaborative action teams with teams from other companies?

_____

_____

_____

_____

Use your sound logic to differentiate between flexible boundaries and blurred boundaries: do you apply personal consideration when defining roles?

_____

_____

_____

_____

Clarifying boundaries: To what degree do you experience blurred boundaries in your organization?

_____

_____

_____

_____

Flexing boundaries: are you working to increase fairness, transparency and involvement in your organization?

_____

_____

_____

_____

Aspiring to satisfaction for all employees: are you working to increase satisfaction among your employees? In what ways. What needs to be improved?

_____

_____

_____

_____

Summary: Listening to your employees. How well do you know each of your employees? How much attention do you devote to them? How can you improve it?

_____

_____

_____

_____

How to manage communication correctly: techniques for improving organizational communication

As I noted in the previous chapter, interactions in general and synergistic interactions in particular, are impacted by the axis of communication and the axis of boundaries. I'll expand on the communication axis less, because a plethora of tools exist for developing groups and teams, or improving communication among employees. Most of them are suitable for the creation of fusing communication. These include communication from the heart, non-violent communication, assertive communication, transformative mediation, and so on. All of these are good tools, which are easily brought into use in the organization. While writing this book, I employed Biodanza, with the management of a logistics start up as a way of improving both the sense of diversity, and communication. I certainly recommend it.

I do want to expand on two tools, however, for the benefit of readers who are less familiar with tools to improve communication. The first is relatively common, the second less so.

The Johari Window

This tool was developed for the purpose of allowing people to get a better understanding of their relationship with themselves and with others. In the course of applying the tool for its original purpose, participants are given a list of nouns from which they choose those which best describe their own personalities, and the personalities of their fellow employees. At the end of the group process, all participants receive colleagues' relevant lists, and can combine this information with their own list. Reviewing the linkages between the nouns chosen by the person her- or himself, and those chosen by colleagues, produces four quadrants, as presented in Graph 3a below.

1. The revealed quadrant: describing what is known to me and to my colleagues
2. The blind quadrant: what my colleagues know but I'm unaware of
3. The secret quadrant, also known as the facade: what I know but hide from my colleagues
4. The unknown quadrant: what neither I nor my colleagues are aware of

The recommended use of this tool is to improve communication in general, and create flexible communication in particular, through attempting to expand the known field, or Arena. The expansion would come about, on one hand, through participants' willingness to share knowledge which they have hidden up until then, which inherently reduces the secret field; and on the other, by encouraging colleagues to offer feedback about the blind field, or Blind Spot. Changes are presented in Graph 3b.

Graph 3a: Johari Window

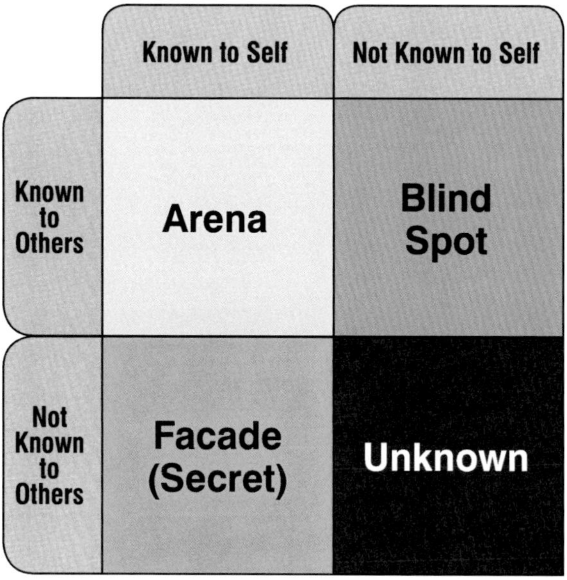

	Known to Self	Not Known to Self
Known to Others	Arena	Blind Spot
Not Known to Others	Facade (Secret)	Unknown

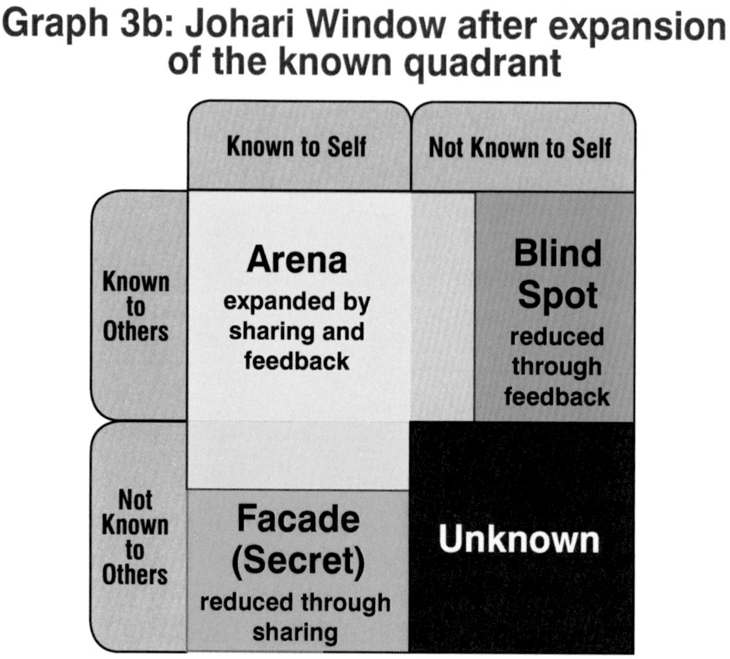

Graph 3b: Johari Window after expansion of the known quadrant

	Known to Self	Not Known to Self
Known to Others	**Arena** expanded by sharing and feedback	**Blind Spot** reduced through feedback
Not Known to Others	**Facade (Secret)** reduced through sharing	**Unknown**

Graph 3b: Johari Window after expansion of the known quadrant

Don't anticipate a fast or sudden change. The process is a spiral, where people learn to open up, on one hand, while giving assertive but non-threatening feedback, on the other. The more comfortable participants feel with the process, the deeper the process will go. I recommended reading "The Johari Window" by Hase, Davies and Dick.

Throughout the book, I've shared personal anecdotes; some might even say they're a bit too personal. I'm actually a very private person who doesn't find it easy to share these stories. But I did so because I'm aware of the connections that personal exposure creates, and I want to encourage the same in organizations. Some organizations still uphold a culture where employees entering the organization's premises, leave their personal lives behind, especially senior management. Joining the spiral of sharing and feedback allows us to be human and vulnerable, and saves us having to direct energy towards maintaining the secrets or the facade at our place of work. But I've also found it appropriate, by using examples from my private life, to demonstrate how expanding the revealed quadrant allows creating closeness that leads to flexing boundaries and fusing communication.

The Listening Circle

The Listening Circle, a tool I'm particularly fond of, is based on folklore from the Native American culture. It's a living example of the synergy I work on in teams and cooperative actions.

The method, as written about by Christina Baldwin, Margaret Wheatley, and others, is a useful tool for developing strong organizational infrastructure based on closeness, trust, group pride, partnership around a common denominator, compassion and mutual assistance, all of which contribute to creating synergy. It generates a rich and honest discourse, which is vital to the essence of the circle. The method reinforces teams, structures relationships, and strengthens respectful communication. It simultaneously infuses participants with a sense of security, calm, attentiveness, willingness to cooperate, and creativity. There is no law of right or wrong: the circle is the outcome of the shared mood.

Rules for conducting a Listening Circle

You can conduct a listening circle in your organization for the purpose of developing discussion on any topic. First, gather your group of employees or team members and invite them to sit together in a circle. Seating must allow everyone to see everyone else's faces. The discussion itself is held while strictly upholding four important rules, as detailed below.

1. The first rule is that in the listening circle, an object

serves as permission to talk. The person holding the object may speak, and no one else is allowed to interrupt. Technically any object can be used, but it's customary to choose something unique or easily identified. Speaking only when holding the object ensures the quality of listening to the speaker, and prevents vocal arguments by other participants from breaking into the speaker's words. If we come into this world with 2 ears but just 1 mouth, perhaps we are meant to do more listening than speaking, even though, in actuality, it's usually the reverse. In most discussions, people zap into others' words and in the end, nothing is understood and nothing is really heard. Using an object to signal permission to speak avoids these types of disruptive situations.

2. The second rule is that the activity calls for "speaking and listening from the heart" where both are carried out respectfully, even if the speaker is different from ourselves. Listeners are required to disconnect from any thoughts, beliefs or preconceived views towards the speaker, and try to link with the words being spoken. In Synergy approach words we call it respect diversity.

3. The third rule is "speaking slim": briefly, and to the point. Many people conduct dialogues because they want to release burdensome thoughts at all costs. This damages the ability to listen. The speaker must therefore focus on what she or he wants to say, which is a way of respecting listeners.

4. The fourth and final rule is to speak spontaneously, without preplanning while someone else in the group is speaking. Listen with close attentiveness to each speaker as that person speaks, and only after she or he has spoken, respond naturally and spontaneously.

Many people find it difficult to express what's on their minds. Make use of breathing techniques to help overcome the barrier. If you've been asked to share and you find it difficult, simply take a deep breath and say the first thing that comes to mind, intuitively, on the topic, without filtering or selecting your comments intellectually.

The more this technique is practiced, the easier it is to use, and more people will join in. An organization that periodically holds listening circles will find them more effective, over the longer term, than one that uses the technique as a one-time or occasional workshop activity. Periodically held listening circles improve interactions among employees, make boundaries more flexible, and help turn fusing into the dominant communication pattern.

Summarizing: any tool for developing teams, group work or improved communication among individuals in the organization will help in managing communication in the organization correctly. Taking advantage of a variety of tools and techniques systematically and over the long term, leads to fusing communication. Feel free to begin using the tools I've described above, or any others with similarly proven outcomes.

Summary and your personal workbook

How can you improve communication among members of your organization? What tools are familiar to you for reinforcing communication, or are already in use in your organization? What can still be improved? Who can carry this out?

_____

_____

_____

_____

_____

How to manage interactions correctly

A quick reminder:
- All 7 forms of interaction exist simultaneously in any organization at any point in time; and
- Each employee or manager experiences the mix of these forms subjectively.

Our role as managers or consultants interested in improving interactions in the organization, is to embed the quality forms in general and synergy in particular, and simultaneously preserve the correct mix of forms, reducing incidents of destructive forms as far as possible. As we aim for synergy, we need to ensure that the quality forms account for at least 70% of the organization's interactions, otherwise the objective will be very difficult to achieve.

We also need to take steps based on the mix of interactions which come to light during the diagnostic stage. In other words, we need to reduce the two destructive forms, being invasion and obscurity, especially in teams or departments where they are experienced at over 7% of the mix, then reduce neutral forms, and lastly, reinforce any quality forms needing a boost.

Reducing the appearance of destructive forms in the organization

Obscurity and invasion tend to characterize states of change, lack of clarity or dissatisfaction with job definitions. Change can be at the organizational or unit level, or even replacing one team member with another.

In general, when blurring of boundaries in the organization increases, we will also find more incidents of invasion, and vice versa. In fact, the two forms often impact each other. When boundaries are blurred, employees or managers have a tendency to invade the role of the other employees.

◑ Reducing the form of obscurity

Reducing the incidence of obscurity means that boundaries have to be clarified, as we've discussed in the section on correctly handling boundaries on page 131.

In Chapter 1 I described my work in a manufacturing plant producing raw materials for the hygiene industry, as the organization was exposed for the first time to clientele in Eastern Europe. As you recall, obscurity derived from the fact that this new region did not fall under the recognized sphere of authority of any sales manager. Such typical situations give rise to blurred boundaries that can quickly foment a power struggle and invasion aimed at taking control of the new role. Fortunately, the general manager identified the situation quickly and found a solution: expanding the areas of authority and responsibility for one manager, who spoke Russian, until a specialized manager could be found to handle the region.

In this example, the decision was reached during a discussion between the sales managers and the CEO, based on mutual consultation and a study of alternatives. This approach would be correct for any similar circumstance where a temporary solution is needed until a permanent one can be implemented. During the discussion, the significance of the change for each of the sales managers was raised, and appropriate small changes in divisions of responsibility and authority were made, geared at minimizing the sense of unfairness. The jointly reached decision was followed up by formally redefining each sales manager's role. In this way, resistance by sales staff was reduced, if any had existed, and no sense of invasion or dissatisfaction developed.

◑ Reducing the form of invasion

After identifying and defining invasion, we need to focus on reducing invasive behaviors. If the average sense of invasion in the organization or unit stands at 2% to 3%, that's an acceptable figure which doesn't require investigation. You should nevertheless examine each questionnaire separately, and wherever you find more than 7% for the invasive interaction, or read examples that turn warning lights on in your thoughts, you must take action.

Why do managers or employees in an organization invade the roles of other people? Numerous reasons can explain the phenomenon, but invasion is always an active move executed by the invader and experienced by the invaded.

This means that reports of invasion will come almost exclusively from the invaded, and the degree of experienced invasion will reflect how destructive the form is to organizational interactions. When invasion is ongoing, counter-invasion will often result, on the basis of "the best defense is attack."

Usually, invaders will explain their actions as responses to situations where, in their view, there was no choice. In fact, it's usually described as some kind of critical or vital situation where the invader just had to intervene and 'help out' with the task at hand, as a way of preventing inevitable damage to the organization. The nature of the invasion, in the invader's view, is essential assistance, needed to save the organization from the impending error or the invaded person's weakness.

I've frequently encountered invasion on the part of a freshly promoted manager. The line of thinking is that if the promoted manager filled the previous role very well, it's only natural that a replacement will not do the job as well, at least initially. Once the interfaced period is complete, each of the managers should concentrate on her or his own role, but in many cases the promoted manager has difficulty in closing the interfacing process. Being closely familiar with the previous role, usually because it was filled for a number of years, the previous manager feels she or he knows how to handle it best. Additionally, cumulative experience makes it easy for the vacating manager to identify the newly appointed manager's deficiencies and problem spots, and easily leads to "stepping into the breach." As invaders often explain, their help comes from a sense of mission.

Another situation giving rise to invasion comes from managers or employees who are unhappy with the boundaries defining their role, or are unsure of them. Wanting to expand areas of authority or protect the role, the invader attacks another person's role, seeking to bring about a change based on the belief that attack is the best defense. This chiefly occurs in organizations with a culture of force, and where invasion is perceived as a legitimate tool for achieving political power. In such organizations, it will be difficult to create high-level synergy, and there is a need to work on change to the organizational culture.

Invasion can also come about because the individual is weak at the professional or managerial level, as exemplified on page 59. in the case of the industrial concern whose VP invaded the role of one of the manufacturing plant managers. The plant manager was a top level professional in his field, with immense and unique knowledge and knowhow of importance to the organization, yet was perceived at the managerial level by other managers and subordinates as weak. This is a dangerous status since it encourages invasion.

◑ The process for reducing invasion between two employees

When attempting to reduce invasion, you have to start by working only with the invader. The goal is to get the invader to understand the implications of invasion, the damage it causes, and how it can be reduced.

This process requires in-depth understanding of the conflict between the two employees. My experience shows that the invader will typically reject the invaded employee's claims, and completely oppose them. This is unfortunate, and means that you'll need to call on all the resources available to you for handling this situation well. I've found that the 7

Forms of Interaction graph for the invasive interaction, on page 50 , can be very useful as you discuss this with your employee. It's what helped me with the industrial concern's VP: the visual graph showing Invasion supported the verbal explanation. For the VP, this was a breakthrough moment that allowed reducing the phenomenon.

The second stage in the process of reducing invasion requires working jointly with invader and invaded. In this meeting your job is to listen closely to what each side is saying and notice how each expresses their feelings: is the spoken language and / or body language assertive, aggressive, quiet and humble, or perhaps making clear efforts to avoid personally attacking the other?

The third stage requires finding an appropriate organizational resolution to the invasive interaction, or the reasons causing it. There is value in not involving the whole team in the details of the reported invasion. Instead, inform the team of the percentages of invasion and obscurity in their unit, and that specific instances of invasion are being handled separately and privately. This enables discreet handling of each case.

In the industrial concern from the earlier example, we successfully reduced invasion by strengthening managers subordinate to the middle range manager, which indirectly reinforced the said manager to the point where the invasive interaction he had experienced almost completely dissipated.

Case Study

The "Happy Waves" company, as we'll call it for our purposes here, produces electronic components for the microwave industry. At the outset of the situation described below, the plant's management team comprised four individuals: the CEO, the Operations Director, the Acquisitions Manager and the Finance Manager. Other managerial functions, such as research and development, marketing, and human resources, were the responsibility of the parent company to which this subsidiary belonged.

The plant was famous for its high level production capabilities, as well as for harmonious relationships among the managers under the direction of the CEO who emphasized cooperation, teamwork, and an upbeat atmosphere. When managers were asked to describe the nature of work with the CEO, they used phrases such as pleasant, easygoing, and "everyone knows their job and carries it out. And whenever necessary, we work as a team and cooperate together."

At a later stage the CEO announced that he would be leaving his role for one in the parent organization. He also shared with the other managers the fact that a replacement had not yet been decided, and mentioned that no decision had been taken concerning whether the new CEO would come from within the current management or from outside.

The CEO's statements upset the balance in management, disrupting the harmony in the relations that had existed, and gave rise to deep conflict among the managerial staff. The acquisitions manager, being the most senior among them, considered himself the natural replacement and began invading the others' roles.

This began a period described by the management team members as one of numerous tense meetings. "We felt unable to freely express ourselves," one said, "and when we did, arguments immediately flared."

From the CEO's perspective at the time, he found it hard to continue the decision making process with his managerial team. "Strong tension was felt," the CEO explained, "and I was forced on any number of occasions to intervene in conflicts among my team members, and take decisions on my own because of the constantly oppositional views."

Eventually, a CEO was appointed from outside the plant. When I was called in to assist the organization, the new CEO had already stepped into the role. My position was defined as restoring the management team's ability to cooperate and improve interactions among them.

After planning my course of action, I began the diagnostic stage by handing out the 7 Forms of Interaction Model questionnaire to the managers. In this case, I asked that they refer to two specific time frames: before the CEO's announcement, and after it.

The findings and written examples showed that 'before' was marked by 85% of Quality forms of interaction. From the moment that the CEO advised the team of his imminent departure, the culture and quality of the interactions shifted drastically, with a reported average of 23% invasion by everybody except the acquisitions manager, who reported a relatively low level of invasion and predominant forms of synergy and interfaced.

After diagnosis, I started out on the corrective process: personal meetings with the acquisitions manager, in which I conveyed the feedback showing high levels of perceived invasion by fellow managers. I also clarified the consequences of his actions. Additionally, I conducted activities geared at team development among the managers, with emphasis on clarifying boundaries, and avoiding mutual invasion and blurring.

A workshop was held for all managers, during which boundaries were redefined. Examples of invasion which I'd been given advance permission to share were aired in front of the whole group. These activities assisted greatly in restoring the harmonious balance that had existed previously, eliminating the invasive interaction that developed in the interim between the CEO's announcement and the new CEO's appointment.

Limiting the appearance of neutral forms in the organization

As shown in Chapter 2, the neutral patterns of no communication and one-way communication tend to develop into negative patterns. It's worth trying to predict where this might happen and take steps to avoid its occurrence. For example, let's say that an employee or manager does not respond to emails in timely fashion. Perhaps initially this behavior is perceived by the person trying to communicate as no connection, or as one-way communication. But if this conduct continues over a long term, it may be perceived as invasion, since the non-responding employee or manager is making it harder for the other party to carry out his or her job, causes that person to feel a subject of derision, and therefore causes the sense of invasion.

If we want to identify these warning signs, we need to analyze examples of one-way communication provided by employees in their questionnaires or interviews and take corrective steps. Further to the example above, we could check with the person who doesn't respond to emails why that's happening, and from there coordinate expectations, such as setting an acceptable maximum time frame for responding, which can lead to improved interactions.

Reducing patterns of no communication
What causes patterns of no communication and how can they be handled?

◑ The development of obscure or invasive forms in the organization
When destructive forms appear in the organization, the people exposed to them frequently respond by breaking off contact, especially when someone feels invaded, threatened or is dissatisfied with the situation. These are not neutral interactions: they are destructive interactions which need to be handled. In fact, the cause that gave rise to them needs handling, but not by disconnection, which only treats the symptom.

◑ Poor communication quality
Physical disconnections caused, for example, by different time zones or shift work, or cultural disconnections which include unfamiliar ways of communicating or language comprehension difficulty, require handling that focuses on improving the quality of communication. Physical communication can be enhanced by appropriate technological solutions; cultural communication can be improved by working on intercultural diversity. In this case, a formal definition of expectations through clear procedures may actually help, even though it rigidifies boundaries.

◑ Work load
Heavy workloads can make it harder to respond to every incoming message, whether from other employees or from

clients. The solution is to handle the cause of the workload, but even prior to that, you can explain to your employee the problem that currently exists, and the effect it is causing, which includes feelings of no communication and disdain.

⦾ Disrespectful behavior

When a manager or fellow employee displays lack of interest or disrespect towards the professional or personal needs of another in the organization, any chance of creating synergy between them is instantly destroyed, since synergy is based first and foremost on respect.

⦾ Reducing patterns of one-way communication

One-way communication is typical of routine interactions such as procedures, or emergency interactions such as orders or commands. Organizations make vast use of procedures, in order to create structured, fixed processes and handle recurring issues. An example would be insurance companies: every category of claim has its clearly structured process, which is used repeatedly. The process contains a large amount of detail, and its requirements are clear to users: what information is needed, how to present it, and so on. For as long as the procedure exists, it represents a pattern of one-way communication, and the employee is required to match the case at hand to the procedure.

I recommend that an organization wishing to create and assimilate procedures should do so by collaborating with its employees. I've often found organizations which have produced highly detailed procedures, but because employees were excluded from the consolidation and writing process, the organization's demand to institute the procedure was perceived by employees as one-way communication if not invasion.

As a result, employees may reject the procedure and avoid using it, even if it makes their work easier. Rejection will be even more pronounced if they feel the procedure is incorrect, unfair, unnecessary, not suited to the requirement it's meant to address, or damaging.

At this point I'd like to return to the example regarding the development of military weapons, described in Chapter 2. Chief of Staff orders are often perceived by in-the-field staff as "so much nonsense." This same attitude can be found in any organization that sets procedures in a top down pathway, without involving those employees who need to work according to the procedures, or listening to their real time experiences.

When a procedure you write is immediately adopted, it's a sure sign you've successfully responded to the situation that the procedure addresses. I strongly recommend collaborating with all parties involved in the procedure's objective. In the case presented in Chapter 2, the procedure was adopted even before it received official authorization. By contrast, a one-way pattern is excellent in cases of emergency, when a clear chain of command is vital and there is no time for collaborative decisions with employees.

We often find that the patterns of no communication and one-way communication link up. The pattern of no communication is perceived as being unfair, since it doesn't allow for feedback or encourage communication. The employee feels that no one is listening and that there's a disconnect between her or him and the organization. That may arouse feelings of invasion or obscurity.

If employees perceive the pattern of one-way communication as damaging or causing problems, you have to handle the situation immediately and improve communication between employees and the organization. This will prevent one-way communication from developing into an interaction of obscurity or invasion.

Another negative manifestation of one-way communication is the appearance of the "playing dumb" phenomenon: the employee becomes used to the idea that she or he isn't really being listened to, therefore does the minimum necessary to survive in the organization. This phenomenon commonly leads to low motivation and low outputs, and particularly to reduced creativity and innovation, both of which are vital to the organization's survival.

Summary: neutral forms are not problematic per se, but can easily spiral down into destructive forms of obscurity and invasion if not handled within a reasonable time frame.

Reinforcing the organization's quality forms

Before I discuss the tools available for reinforcing your organization's quality forms, it's worth summarizing the characteristics shared by the three quality forms shown in the 7 Forms of Interaction Model:

1. All three quality forms have clearly defined and agreed boundaries.
2. All three quality forms are noteworthy for recognizing the importance of diversity and relating with respect to that diversity.
3. All three quality forms can be improved with training, team development and enhanced management skills.

After reducing the scope of destructive and neutral forms in your organization, it's time to focus on strengthening the quality forms, based on the percentages they were allocated in the diagnostic process questionnaires.

Reinforcing quality forms in general, and synergy in particular, requires operating along two axes: the axis for flexing boundaries, and the axis for communication improvement. When it comes to quality forms, these two axes are interlinked, one supporting the other. They can't always be differentiated, nor is there any need to: activities towards improving communication enable flexing boundaries, which in turn promotes improved communication, and so on.

I will now present a range of tools and processes which I've implemented with clients when reinforcing synergy in their organizations. Your organization should adopt tools and processes best suited to your purposes, and even develop additional unique tools. Note how some tools are suitable for the focused effort at the stage of assimilating the synergy method, others focus on reinforcing synergy, and yet others are suitable only for very large organizations.

Tools and processes for reinforcing synergy

Simultaneous to writing this book, I began assisting the Tel Aviv Municipality's Corporations Bureau Director, in reviewing a methodology for improving synergy among city corporations. My thanks to him for his help, in return, with preparing the list of tools.

Integrating synergy into vision, values and work plans

Integrating the synergy approach into the organizational vision is meant, among other purposes, to link employees to the organization's vision. There's no doubt that believing in the organization's purpose, sense of mission, and the importance of its objectives (particularly when those are urgent and critical), cause an organization's members to harness their abilities to the process of creating synergy, without surrendering to ego-based considerations.

Below are values which I recommend that you infuse into your organizational vision and your organization's ethical code:

- Acknowledging diversity and multiculturalism among employees and clients
- Respecting employees and clients with special needs
- Transparency
- Fairness and decency
- Believing that the group's solution will always be better than that of the individual

For example, following the merger of two banks, the value of synergy was introduced as one of the new bank's core values.

Writing the vision down, and periodically checking or reevaluating it, are important actions towards maintaining employees' involvement with the organization's activities. You can do this through simple visual means such as having it appear on computer screens as a screen saver, as a background in meetings, integrated into internal organizational documents, and on the company website.

Single year and multiyear work plans distributed throughout the organization can promote synergy, and processes of feedback and review can ensure that the vision is in fact being realized and implemented in real time by organization members. The review may include a decision that in their annual or quarterly reports, all managers must present the steps they have taken to reinforce synergy in their unit.

Please note the need to "walk the talk." If senior managers do not behave according to the organization's norms or values, employees might perceive it as an invasion.

Steps to increase transparency, involvement and fairness which assist flexing boundaries

Beyond defining the values of transparency, involvement and fairness as representing the organization's values, it's important to adopt tangible steps towards reinforcing and implementing them, such as:

1. Using defined targets in areas which improve synergy in the organization's ongoing management, such as targets for the number of team discussions per month, for topic-specific training, etc.
2. Increasing transparency in management, chiefly in organizational knowledge retrieval: contributions to creating and sharing knowledge of value to the organization, recurring use of knowledge, and

remuneration (not necessarily monetary) for contributing to organizational knowledge.

These kinds of tools create a culture of learning, and encourage knowhow and ideas sharing. They also encourage flexing boundaries and reducing activities based on ego or organizational micro-politics.

Encouraging informal interactions in your organization

Conducting informal interactions among members of your organization will help you expand the revealed quadrant appearing in the Johari Window on page 145. Consider holding a fixed weekly informal meeting where personal content can be raised, such as celebrating birthdays or family events, enjoying refreshments, and praising personal or team achievements of excellence. Get-togethers of this kind create a warmer family atmosphere and further flex boundaries.

Informal interactions can be encouraged by publicizing personal information about employees across intra-organizational media channels such as the weekly bulletin, the shared work site, and more, or posting group photos of employees in locations within the organization or group outings, and more.

Wellbeing events such as parties, shared recreational activities, and weekends away with or without partners can also be used, but they have to be handled carefully, since some employees may experience them as invasive of their leisure time and personal choices. For this reason, I recommend checking with your employees about the kinds of activities they prefer, and when they want to hold them, rather than setting commitments with too much rigidity.

Case Study

Earlier in this book I described my work with a PR company which brought in a new CEO, replacing the company proprietor who had filled this role up to then. As part of the process, the company underwent a series of significant changes to its organizational structure: switching to working in teams, changes to definitions of managers' roles, recasting the salary scale, and more.

The entire period in which these changes were taking place was characterized by informal interactions such as weekly meetings, parties and outings. The company was experiencing growth, doubled its office space and created a "Wellbeing Room" for its employees, a place where it was possible just to chill for a while, on work time. The room was equipped to encourage interactions among employees, while simultaneously promoting creative thinking and relaxation.

The move helped create friendly relations among employees, the majority of whom were new to the company. Cooperation of this kind, especially in an organization focused on public relations work which is strongly based on talent, is not trivial, but it can have a vital positive impact. In this way, the company's transition through essential changes was relatively easy, and additionally improved outputs, particularly increases in the number of clients and in client satisfaction.

Encouraging informal interactions by familiarizing with other organizational units

By holding meetings between employees with different roles or between different organizational units, you can lessen the feeling of rigid boundaries, and promote synergistic interactions. These meetings can be formal activities such as units hosting other units, holding office meetings jointly with various units and purposely changing the location of the meeting and the discussion topics, holding meetings in field unit offices and not only in the head office, and so on. This recommendation is particularly suited to large or decentralized organizations with several branches.

Encouraging formal interactions through initiated forum encounters

I recommend holding fixed forums with functionaries who meet periodically. This could be in the form of study forums which take on a different topic each time and are operated according to best practices, with the activities documented at whatever level of detail you find suitable. This tool is suitable for organizations with several units which carry out the same processes. It allows learning from diversity by sharing how each unit carries out the process, which allows other units to choose tactics or methods that are worth adopting.

Appointing a designated employee as "synergy trustee"

You should encourage an employee to be the designated torch bearer for maintaining synergy in the organization. That person should ensure that the process of embedding synergy is implemented and maintained in your organization. Generally this is an additional function to the employee's primary role, but one which requires your employee to undergo training that will allow her or him to facilitate synergistic processes.

Appointing a "synergy trustee" ensures that companies which have made use of a professional consultant's services can carry on the consultant's guidelines. For example, in the Hadassah Women's Organization, the appointment and training of synergy facilitators assisted continued embedding of the synergistic language and method. This ensured that the principles and practices would be carried on to additional volunteers along a continuum of activities. The organization's management was also assisted by the synergy approach when planning new projects, especially those requiring integration of volunteers from both groups of women.

A mechanism for settling disputes

Having a mechanism in place for settling disputes allows bridging and resolving conflicts in certain situations, thus strengthening cooperation among individual employees or between diverse units in the organization. The benefits increase when the mechanism is correctly structured and doesn't cause either side to experience invasion. The mechanism can be led by an employee from the human resources department, or any other neutral employee in the organization who has the appropriate standing and has received training to maintain synergy or mediate conflicts.

A dispute or conflict resolution mechanism allows both sides to raise issues around the conflict for discussion, while agreeing to accept the chosen solution. The very existence of such a mechanism reinforces the synergy approach in your organization, by representing authentic efforts at understanding the conflict's cause in terms of no communication, invasion, or blurred boundaries. Try for a synergistic resolution based on my recommendations for handling excessive ranges of destructive or neutral form, which appears previously in this chapter.

The debriefing processes

Any organization wanting to improve its synergy, large organizations in particular, should adopt investigative or debriefing processes which encourage reaching clear conclusions. This promotes learning, instead of looking for where to cast blame.

In one municipality I worked with, the process was called "Smart-Up" rather than formal, weighty labels such as "debrief" or "investigation." Playing on the concept of startups and their creative focus in finding solutions to societal needs, a smartup discussion emphasizes the learning curve and positive outcomes, particularly from the perspective of employees. It carries none of the negative connotations perceived by employees vis-à-vis words like "investigation" or "review." In any event, the 7 Forms of Interaction Model and the language of synergy serve as valuable platforms for investigating problem spots.

Because this is an internal process which is usually carried out by fellow team or department members, it's important to pay attention to whoever is conducting the process and ensure that focus is placed on reaching conclusions without getting drawn into criticism or arousing additional conflicts.

Balancing the process: differentiation / integration, decentralization / centralization

Many organizations tend to operate like pendulums. They experiment with decentralization and differentiation for a while. This allows for delegating top-down authority while promoting greater closeness with clients, and facilitates operating in diverse niches. But these actions also cause a sense of lost control in senior management and head offices, wasted resources, and errors. Often, management will reinstate integration and centralization to their former levels.

Operating according to the synergy approach provides the organization with tools for coping with the consequences of these processes, including preserving clear boundaries which are sufficiently flexible to allow decentralization or differentiation without losing control at HQ level. The solution might be to decentralize and differentiate implementation processes while centralizing policy making and control processes. (For the article scan the QR on the back cover).

Balancing functions in the organization

Every organization contains functions which encourage rigidifying boundaries, and functions that encourage flexing them.

◐ **Functions that rigidify** include control, review, legal consultancy, procedures, structured processes, and coordination via standardized inputs and outputs.

⑩ **Functions that help flex** boundaries include human resources, with particular focus on management development, training, and employee wellbeing activities, organizational development, R&D, client liaison, services, marketing, strategy, and direct coordination.

If we want to strengthen the synergy form in the organization, we need to be aware of these diverse functions and find a way to balance them. This usually occurs through mechanisms that grant authority to managers and employees in functions that rigidify boundaries by focusing on tools that encourage synergy.

The case study on page 14, describing my personal experience with the Japanese airline, reflects the right balance between functions: the Japanese are known for scrupulous adherence to structured procedures, yet a sufficient ability to flex boundaries made it possible to agree to my request.

Summary: I briefly presented a range of tools that can help reinforce quality interactions in general, and the synergy approach in particular, in your organization. You should also feel free to introduce any other tools you find suitable to these goals and to your organizational culture and managerial needs.

At this point, I want to reiterate the importance of acknowledging diversity among your employees, and understanding that any process, tool or action will only ever match the needs of some employees. This is why I recommend being in touch with your employees in real time, and asking them to share their views on finding solutions to their issues. Your staff and managers are the most important assets your organization holds. The gains of managing these assets with the synergy approach make the effort worthwhile.

Summary and your personal workbook

What actions can you take towards improving management of interactions?

Reducing destructive forms of obscurity and invasion

_____

_____

_____

_____

Reducing neutral forms of hierarchy and patterns of no communication

_____

_____

_____

_____

Reinforcing quality forms of interdependence, interfaced and synergy

_____

_____

_____

_____

Tools for creating quality forms and synergy that you want your organization to adopt (not necessarily only from those I have recommended)

_____

_____

_____

_____

And lastly - What's the next step?

It's over, but it has only just begun: the book is reaching its end, and your work will now begin.

In this book, I've presented the synergy approach for improving organizational interactions, and given you a taste of the synergy assimilation process, through a variety of examples that will help you implement synergy in your organization.

Our first step was to define organizational synergy.

Next, we looked at basic concepts such as diversity, boundaries and communication. We mapped the 7 Forms of Interaction Model and expanded on the synergy form, offered guidelines and recommendations for reducing destructive forms, and ways for improving the productive forms in general, with a special focus on synergy. The synergy questionnaire was provided for you to practice on, and we examined examples of synergy and authentic case studies.

Now the ball's in your court. I want you to give yourself permission to be gutsy, take the plunge, and dream of creating a new, synergistic reality in your organization. Think about the most important message you've gained from the book, and how you can translate what you've learned into practical applications: What's your immediate move as of tomorrow? A week from now? Next month? Half a year from now, and in a year? Who will your partners be in this process, and how will you get them excited about synergy?

Most important of all, what does "organizational synergy" mean for you? What kind of new reality do you want to see in your organization? It might be a large scale switch that replaces much or all of the current organizational culture, or a relatively modest change such as creating a reality where board or management meetings are more productive because attendees are listening better to each other. It may also be finding the reality that ensures that decisions reached at meetings get effectively implemented because it has become easier to harness board members or managers to take on new projects, and more.

Your personal workbook: What's your VISION?

_____

_____

_____

_____

_____

In the introduction I asked you to write down statements, complaints or criticisms that you frequently hear from employees or managers as a result of situations which indicate lack of synergy in the organization. If you were to interview employees several months from now, after you've had some time to work on embedding synergy, what are the statements you'd like to hear from your employees and managers?

Your personal workbook: What STATEMENTS would you like to hear from your employees?

_____

_____

_____

_____

_____

Whether you wrote a clear vision for creating synergy or want to write it later, I do want to remind you that improving synergy in the organization is a fascinating process that can lead to impressive improvements and achievements at the levels of the individual employee, the team, the unit and the whole organization. But keep in mind that the process is not a simple one. It can sometimes be very challenging, because it alters your organization's managerial language and culture: not only does it make the organization more open and less political, it promotes shared activity and demotes competition.

Your success in embedding the synergy approach will lead to essential changes that will be felt in increased client satisfaction and employee satisfaction, in your organization's atmosphere, in the indexes for work process quality, outputs and profits, and any other index you want to define as a synergistic goal for promoting a new reality in that area.

Your ability to bring change to your organization depends on your ability to assimilate changes in yourself, adopt the terminologies, the work processes and the principles this book has presented. It also depends on how much you invest in everyone in your organization, which reflects your success through their assimilation of the synergy method. If you keep in mind that each employee will take independent decisions about her or his rate of learning and adoption of synergistic approaches and thinking, you'll understand just how critical and crucial is your role as the leader responsible for your organization's wellbeing.

Use this book as your basis for familiarizing with the synergy method, practicing it in the workbook sections, and setting out on a new path to a synergistic organization.

*

Here are a few more ways you can expand your knowledge on the synergy method:

- ◍ Reread the book and practice the exercises
- ◍ Join my website www.ben-yshai.com and enjoy the updates I publish on synergy
- ◍ Send me your questions about the process via the website's Contact Me tab. That way we can keep up the synergy between us, continue learning, practicing, sharing our experiences, and promoting synergy in the organization, in society, and in the world.

The more I delve into organizational synergy, the more areas I find where it is possible to benefit from the method: in mergers or acquisitions, in third sector organizations such as not-for-profits and social enterprises, in small businesses, in startups, and more. I'll be referring to them in greater detail through articles, books, conferences and workshops that aim to encourage shared thinking by people or organizations operating in the same field. If any of these areas interest you or are relevant to you, and you want to take part in the process of research and implementation of synergy assimilation in your business or organization, I'd be happy to hear from you.

Wishing you success,
Dr. Rami Ben-Yshai

Acknowledgments

This book is nothing short of synergy in the making. It was helped along its way by many wonderful people, to each one of whom I am deeply grateful, and in particular to:

Professor Shaul Fuchs, Professor Yitzhak Samuel, Professor Ilan Meshulam, Dr. Rita Aloni, Ayala Groen, Telma Ehrman, Avi Katko, and Uri Moses, who all helped with reading and whose comments were insightful and to the point, helping me fine-hone and sharpen the ideas presented here.

Special thanks are due to my teachers, students and clients, all partners to developing the synergy method that serves as the foundation for the theory and practical application.

Warmest thanks to my family and friends, who are there with me on my journey, are a source of strength, a compass when needed, and a mirror like no other.

References

Baldwin, C. (1998) *Calling the circle: The first and future culture.* New York: Bantam Books

Ben-Shahar, Tal. (2012) *Choose the life you want: The mindful way to happiness.* The Experiment Press

Collins, Jim. (2001) *From good to great: Why some companies make the leap... and others don't.* Harper Collins

Fuchs, S. (1998) *The psychology of resistance to change.*

Hase, Steward; Alan Davies; Bob Dick (1999). *The Johari Window and the Dark Side of Organisations.* Southern Cross University

Malone, T. W., Laubacher, R., & Morton, M. S. (2003) *Inventing the Organizations of the 21st Century.* MIT Press

Robbins, S. (1993) *Organizational behavior.* Englewood Cliffs, N.J.: Prentice Hall: (See chapter on Decision Making)

Woolley, A. W., Chabris, C. F., Pentland, A., Hashmi, N., & Malone, T. W. (2010). *Evidence for a collective intelligence factor in the performance of human groups.* Science, 330(6004), 686-688

Wheatley, M. (2002) Turning to one another: *Simple conversations to restore hope to the future.* San Francisco, CA: Berrett-Koehler Publishers, Inc.

Zimmerman, Jack (author) & Coyle, Virginia (collaborator). (1996) *The way of council.* Bramble Books

BONUS ARTICLE

How do the terms Uniformity and Uniqueness supplement the concept of Diversity and encourage the creation of synergy?

Diversity is the primary area related to in my book. But as an expansion to the concept presented in the Introduction, this bonus article, explores two additional concepts linked to diversity, which complement and supplement it, and encourage the creation of synergy: uniformity, and uniqueness.

They are worth the extra attention due to the confusion that sometimes arises in understanding the differences which define them, and the need to pinpoint each one's contribution to understanding the synergy approach.

Demonstrating uniformity and uniqueness are the following examples, accompanied by graphs that clarify how these concepts manifest in an organization based on the synergy approach.

Adam, Céline and Sayed are good friends who've all recently completed their university studies in Electronic Engineering. They were all recruited, on the same day and together, by a company involved in development, production and sale of electronic components.

Adam is married, is the father of one infant, was an average student, but is very dedicated and industrious. He was slotted into the support department, where most employees are integrated and handle the company's various client sites. There's almost no contact between the employee and the home company. The scope of Adam's work hours is important to him because he plans on having more children and wants to be involved in raising them.

Céline and Sayed, by contrast, are excellent students who were integrated into the R&D department. Céline, single, wants to continue her studies, and views the company as a short term work place. Its primary purpose from her perspective is a chance to gain experience that will assist in her continued education. For Sayed, also single, proving himself in the company is important because his applications for several other jobs were rejected despite being an excellent student.

The R&D department is a small unit. All its members are engineers, most with Masters Degrees. The atmosphere is warm, with great informal relations and high levels of satisfaction.

When they started work, Adam, Céline and Sayed, along with other new employees, were invited to the company's familiarization course, which presents the company's culture, values and vision. Part of the course was devoted to consolidating the new employees in the organization, and introducing them to the company's framework of friendly interactions.

Let's take a look at how the three friends integrated in their new workplace, a company which places high value on the synergy approach by relating to the concepts of diversity, uniformity and uniqueness.

1. Diversity

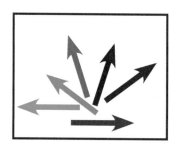

The Concept of Diversity
Graph 1: Diversity

As we saw in the Introduction, diversity is an expression of difference relative to certain aspects, or a lack of uniformity. According to the synergy approach, diversity manifests in the organization through cultural, social and professional differences. The concept of diversity is represented in Graph 1 by arrows of various colors, each one representing an employee, unit or department having an essentially different nature to that of any other employee, unit or department. Similarly, in the description above, the differences among the three friends manifest at several levels: the unit each was slotted into, their genders, their nationalities, their personal goals and ambitions, their professional qualities, and more.

An organization that promotes synergy acknowledges the diversity of each employee, as seen in Graph 1. None of the employees, units or departments are represented by the same color. In other words, there is no uniformity. The organization allows each entity to feel comfortable with their diversity at all levels, including personality traits, knowing that it is these diverse elements which help the organization create the strongest shared reality.

In other words, an organization that promotes synergy will aim for employees who are differentiated from each other in numerous ways, in order to optimally benefit from what each one offers. Yet this organization should simultaneously look for uniformity in aspects such as vision, goals, work plan, and so on.

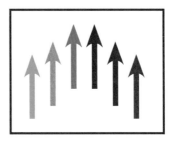

The Concept of Uniformity
Graph 2: Uniformity

Organizations often aspire to uniformity by defining joint goals or a joint vision that serves as a signpost for employees of a specific department or the whole organization. It is considered a way of encouraging employees to focus their energies in a specific direction. The unifying factor may also be defined as a shared interest, achievable target in a specified time frame, or shared work procedures.

But a shared goal can sometimes encourage employees in the same unit or department to forego their need to express their diversity, at least during the hours they spend in the organization, and orient their natures and efforts towards the shared interest. The concept of uniformity, represented in Graph 2, shows that the arrows are still in different colors, acknowledging the diversity among employees, units or department, but they are all pointing the same direction and operating within the framework of uniformity.

In the case of our three friends, Adam, Céline and Sayed, the organization sought to attain uniformity by sending all three to their shared familiarization course. But the course should not suggest that they need to forego their dreams, goals, or personal traits which shape their diversity. Instead, the organization is inviting them to contribute from their diverse traits.

3. Uniqueness

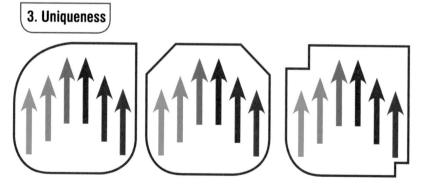

The concept of uniqueness
Graph 3: Uniqueness

According to the synergy approach, the concept of uniqueness is an expression of difference that complements the concept of diversity.

Uniqueness may manifest in a specific department or unit and even among individual employees, such as when employees hold unique knowledge. Although an organizational vision expresses the concept of uniformity, an organization promoting synergy will allow each department or unit to express its uniqueness while operating within the organizational vision.

Members of the team, unit or department can adopt characteristics that unify and differentiate them from other organizational department, especially if these characteristics assist them in achieving the department's goals.

The concept of uniformity is usually implemented in complex, large to mid-range organizations with a wide variety of products and / or services. As long as the unit's or department's uniqueness does not contradict the organization's vision, its uniqueness supports the creation of synergy. Uniqueness differentiates the group and contributes to a sense of cohesiveness among the group's members, while simultaneously reinforcing them. Graph 3 shows how each group or team operates within a unifying yet unique framework of its own, and all groups function within the uniform framework of the organization as a whole.

Summary: when the organization operates according to the synergy method, and allows the concepts of uniformity and uniqueness to simultaneously exist, they reinforce the synergy pattern further. After assimilating synergy in the organization, and once the concepts of uniformity, uniqueness and diversity are implemented, cognitive collective synergy is created, which allows collective insightfulness to rise to the surface. This is precisely when we see an increase in the occurrence of creative, innovative thinking as a direct result of the synergistic environment which enables diversity to manifest.

The synergy method acknowledges the value of diversity and encourages its expression by recognizing the importance of uniformity and uniqueness.

Correctly managing diversity through clear boundaries is the basis for successfully creating synergy, starting from individual diversity in skills, strengths, and tendencies and up to cultural and national diversity. Uniformity, by contrast, is created when the synergy approach is implemented through quality communication. The three concepts of diversity, uniformity and uniqueness complement each other, and encourage synergy in an organization where boundaries are correctly defined, yet flexible, and when quality communication exists among all parties in the organization: employees, departments and management. If you'd like to know more about this subject, I recommend reading: "Inventing the Organizations of the 21st Century."

Made in the USA
San Bernardino, CA
19 February 2019